SCHOLASTIC

Grades K–2

Pick a Poem!

300+ Kid-Pleasing Poems for All the Topics You Teach

by Helen H. Moore & friends

New York ○ Toronto ○ London ○ Auckland ○ Sydney
New Delhi ○ Mexico City ○ Hong Kong ○ Buenos Aires

Teaching *Resources*

Dedication
To my very own
Kim Catalano

Acknowledgments
Many, many thanks go to Liza Charlesworth, my patient, talented,
and dedicated editor and dear, dear friend. Also to Virginia Dooley of
Scholastic Professional Books.

Thanks, also, to the very first, anonymous writers of poetry in English for
children, who often go by the pseudonym "Mother Goose."

ISBN: 978-0-545-15046-0
Design by Grafica
Illustrations by Bob Alley, Teresa Anderko, Paige Billin-Frye, Maxie Chambliss, Steve Cox, Rusty Fletcher, Patrick Girouard, James Hale, Doug Jones, Anne Kennedy, Kelly Kennedy, Anthony Lewis, Tammie Lyon, Mike Moran, Jeff Shelly, Terry Sirrell, George Toufexis, Rebecca Thornburgh, Richard Torrey, Bari Weissman, Jenny Williams, Jane Yamada

4 5 6 7 8 9 10   40   19 18 17 16 15 14 13

Table of Contents

Whatever the Weather

Best Me I Can Be!

Family, Friends, Community

Letter Learning

Shapes, Colors & Primary Concepts

On the Farm

Mammals & More

Remarkable Reptiles & Awesome Amphibians

Birds, Birds, Birds!

Creepy Crawlies

In the Deep Blue Sea

Earth & Beyond

Science & Nature

Food & Fun

Mother Goose & Classic Rhymes

Introduction

Why Teach With Poetry?

To learn to love poetry is to learn to love language, and even very simple, sometimes silly, rhyming poetry, the kind in this book, can open the world of words to your students. Children in grades K–2 are very much in love with language learning; they love learning words, knowing words, inventing their own words, and of course, speaking words. You can use this love of language to engage young children in all sorts of themes and subjects by introducing poetry into your classroom practice—with results that will delight both you and the children in your class.

Rhyming poetry has a built-in fun factor. Children enjoy rhyming words—learning them and saying them, and especially mastering the ability to read them. Rhyming poetry, with its predictable qualities, makes it easy for emergent and early readers to demonstrate reading mastery of age-appropriate material. Copy and distribute these poems to students. Encourage children to color the illustrations and add to the poems with their own lines, rhymes, and images, then make them into classroom charts and chants. Let children point out the silliness of some of the images, and encourage them to create similar poems themselves; their imagination should be the only limit.

Poetry connects readers to language at a very high level—a level that employs the deep, imagistic qualities of language as well as its sensory qualities. It encourages the reader to think, make connections, and explore his or her own thoughts. In order to make sense to the reader, a poem must be grammatical. It must be exact, and in order to be worth reading—especially for a very young audience—it must be fun. It's my hope you will take advantage of these qualities of poetry in your classroom.

Good poetry should be specific, should stretch the reader's vocabulary, and engage the reader's five senses. The simple poems in this book meet your students "where they're at," but stretch them a little, too. They are designed with the needs and abilities of young readers in mind, and with you in mind as well, covering topics and themes you are likely to teach—from sight words to the presidency to the seasons of the year to animals and their habits (and habitats) to the life cycle of a pumpkin seed. Use them any way you like: to start a theme or topic, as bulletin-board content, or as reading material in themselves. Reading and reciting poetry often inspires writing poetry; you can also use these poems to start your students writing their own poems. The possibilities are limitless!

—Helen H. Moore

School Days

Start of School

Summer was fun,
Summer was cool,
Now we're going
Back to school!

Fire drills, and lunchtime spills,
And learning everything…
Now that it's time
To go to school,
It makes me want to sing!

—Helen H. Moore

New Friends

New friends,
New friends,
I-love-you friends,
Laugh-until-your-face-turns-blue friends,
I love all my friends!
Short friends,
Tall friends,
Let's-play-ball friends,
I just know I love them all, friends,
I love all my friends!

—Helen H. Moore

Countdown

Climb aboard the rocket ship,
It's time to fly away.
We're launching into space,
To start our busy day!
So let's begin the countdown,
We'll start with number ten.
And when the day is done,
We'll come back to Earth again!
10…9…8…7…6…5…4…3…2…1…
BLASTOFF!

—Pamela Chanko

My Teacher

My teacher is kind,
My teacher is smart,
My teacher loves teaching
Down deep in her heart.

My teacher is fair,
My teacher is fun,
She teaches us everything
Under the sun.

—*Helen H. Moore*

Crayons

I had a box of crayons,
All shiny, straight, and new.
I lent a friend one crayon.
And—oops!—it broke in two!

My friend said he was sorry,
But I said, "I don't care,"
'Cause now we both can color
With one crayon that we share!

—*Helen H. Moore*

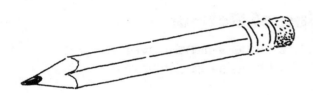

New Pencils

Long and thin
with pointy tops
waiting in my
pencil box—
yellow pencils
(Number 2)
do just what I tell them to.
They can draw
Both straight and wavy,
Draw a boat
Or draw a navy!
(Even draw French fries with gravy!)
New pencils, I love you!

—*Helen H. Moore*

Jiggle, Wiggle, and Giggle

It's time to get the sillies out,
So come and join the fun.
We're getting all the giggles out,
We'll wiggle 'til we're done!

Roll your head in circles,
Then flip it side to side.
Now jiggle both your shoulders,
And stretch your arms up high.

Wiggle all your fingers.
Give your ears a tug.
Twist your waist, bend back and forth,
And give yourself a hug!

Wiggle all your toes-ies
Then gently run in place.
Stick your tongue out all the way,
And make a silly face!

Wiggle, jiggle every part.
Be a silly clown!
Now take a breath…and let it out.
It's time to settle down.

—Pamela Chanko

End of School

School time's almost over.
School time's almost done.

We've had a lot of learning,
We've had a lot of fun.

We'll say goodbye to teachers,
We'll put our books away,
Our school year is over now,
It's summertime—let's play!

—Helen H. Moore

School Bus

Vroom, vroom, vroom—
Hop on, there's room,
On the shiny yellow school bus
That is taking us to school!

And when the school day ends,
We'll ride with all our friends
On the shiny yellow school bus
That will take us home again!

—Helen H. Moore

Sensational Seasons & Magical Months

Winter, Spring, Summer, Fall

Winter, Spring
Summer, Fall.
Which do you
Like best of all?

Winter's cold.
Summer's hot.
Springtime's green,
And Fall is not!

I can't decide.
I like them all,
Winter, Spring,
Summer, Fall!

—Helen H. Moore

Four Seasons

Spring is showery, flowery, bowery.
Summer is hoppy, croppy, poppy.
Autumn is wheezy, sneezy, freezy.
Winter is slippy, drippy, nippy.

—Anonymous

Calendar Poem

Thirty days hath September,
April, June, and November;
February has twenty-eight alone,
All the rest have thirty-one,
Excepting leap year, that's the time
When February's days are twenty-nine.

—Author Unknown

Weekday Warm-Up!

Seven days are in a week.
That's seven days to play.
Seven different ways to move—
One for every day!
Mondays are for marching.
Tuesdays are for tiptoeing.
Wednesdays are for waving.
Thursdays are for thumping.
Fridays are for flapping.
Saturdays are for stretching.
Sundays are for skipping.
Seven different ways to move,
Seven ways to play.
Now, tell me by the way you move—
What day is today?

    —Pamela Chanko

Switcheroo Seasons

Summer is hot
And winter is not,
Unless of course,
You live in a spot,
Where summer is cold
And winter is hot.

    —Helen H. Moore

Fall Is Here!

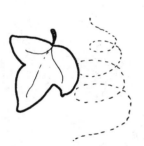

Fall is here.
Another year
Is coming to an end.
Summer's finished,
Summer's gone,
Winter's round the bend.
Fall is piles of crunchy leaves,
Orange, gold, and red.
Fall is sweaters with long sleeves,
Fall is football,
Fall is pumpkins,
Fall is where summer ends.
And fall is coming back to school
And seeing all my friends.

    —Helen H. Moore

Wild Winter Weather

Put your hands together
For wild, winter weather,
For piles of snow,
And winds that blow,
And temperatures
So very low!
For mittens and jackets, and boots so warm
They keep us snug in a wintry storm.

—Helen H. Moore

Summertime!

Today's the day
Vacation starts
It's gonna be
So great!
We'll swim and play
And laugh all day,
Toss balls and roller-skate.
Ride bikes and run,
Have lots of fun,
And get to say up late!
And just in time,
Before we tire
Of all the summer fun,
The day will come
For to hear
"Wake up! School has begun!"

—Helen H. Moore

Spring Has Sprung!

Spring has sprung, and
How do I know?
A springtime birdie
Told me so.

Spring has sprung,
The grass is growing, and
Springtime flowers will
Soon be showing.

—Helen H. Moore

A Year of Months

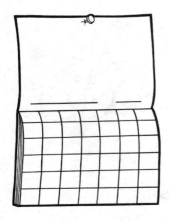

In January, it may snow.
In February, cold winds blow.
In March, a kite is flying high.
In April, rain clouds fill the sky.
In May, the seeds begin to sprout.
In June, the insects crawl about.
July is when the sun shines bright.
In August, stars light up the night.
September means it's back to school.
October means the air gets cool.
We rake November leaves, and then
December—it gets cold again!

—*Pamela Chanko*

January

Snowing, blowing, January
Starts the year off cold.
We say "hello" to the New Year now,
And "goodbye" to the old.

—*Helen H. Moore*

February

Poor, poor February,
Cold and dark and short.
Every other month has lots
Of days for fun and sport.
But February isn't long,
Its days are cold and wet.
And it's as short as any month
Can ever, ever get!

—*Helen H. Moore*

March

Forward, March
And welcome Spring,
When bunnies bounce
And birds all sing!

When March winds blow
The winter away,
They get the world ready for
April and May.

—*Helen H. Moore*

April

An April day can bring us rain
And rain can bring us flowers.
No wonder people like to see
Those rainy April showers!

—*Helen H. Moore*

May

May I say
That I like May?
I wish every day
Was a May kind of day—
With growing grass
And buzzing bees,
With blowing breezes
And flowering trees!

—*Helen H. Moore*

June

There's no other moon
Like a moon in June,
Gold and round
As a balloon.
I'd like to see
A June moon, soon.

—*Helen H. Moore*

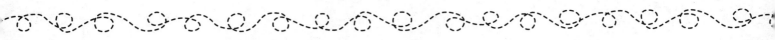

July

Oh, me!
Oh, my!
It's already
July!
How fast
the year
Is whizzing by,
Just like the fireworks we spy
In the nighttime sky
In warm July.

—*Helen H. Moore*

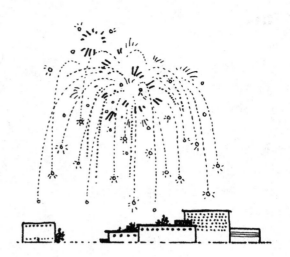

September

September means goodbye to swimming
In the swimming pool.
We put on our September clothes
As we go back to school.
Goodbye to shorts and bathing suits,
We won't wear 'til next year.
It's time for sweaters, hats, and boots,
September time is here!

—*Helen H. Moore*

August

When the sun is so hot,
The streets turn to dust,
Then it really must
Be the month of August.

—*Helen H. Moore*

October

When leaves are falling to the ground,
And pumpkins sprout all over town,
We know October's come around.

—Helen H. Moore

November

Days are growing shorter,
Days are colder, too,
November means Thanksgiving—that
Means treats for me and you.
Like roasted turkey,
Mashed potatoes,
pumpkin pies and such.
I really love November
And the foods I love so much.

—Helen H. Moore

December

Lights and decorations,
Candles and trees,
Menorahs, Kinaras,
December has these.

Snowflakes and starshine
As the year ends,
December's the month
For family and friends.

—Helen H. Moore

Happy Holidays

Birthday Name Song

(Sing to the tune of "Bingo")

Someone's _____ years old today,
And _____ is his/her name-o!
(Spell out name three times, clapping each letter.)
Yes, _____ is his/her name-o!

—Pamela Chanko

If Your Birthday Is Today

(Sing to the tune of "If You're Happy and You Know It")

If you're _____ years old today, clap your hands!
If you're _____ years old today, clap your hands!
If your birthday is today, and you want to shout "Hooray!"
If you're _____ years old today, clap your hands!

—Pamela Chanko

Happy Birthday!

Today's the day,
We get to say,
We're happy you were born—
       Hooray!

    —Helen H. Moore

It's Time to Celebrate

(Sing to the tune of "Farmer in the Dell")

It's time to celebrate
A friend who's really great,
_____ is _____ years old today,
It's such a special date!

    —Pamela Chanko

Three Black Cats

(Sing to the tune of "Three Blind Mice")

Three black cats, three black cats,
Hear how they mew, hear how they mew.
They crossed my path one Halloween night,
And tried to give me a terrible fright!
But all those cats ran right out of sight,
When I said, "BOO!"

    —Pamela Chanko

Halloween

In the starry dark
of the autumn sky,
a ghost-shaped cloud
went drifting by.

That cloudy ghost
Looked down to see,
A kid-shaped shadow
That belonged to me.

My shadow and the cloud
Gave each other quite a fright,
Then we shared a laugh together
On a Halloween night.

    —Helen H. Moore

Who's Who on Halloween

I never know who I might meet
When I go out to trick-or-treat.
Witches with their pointy hats,
Spooky cats and scary bats.
Ghosts and goblins saying "Boo,"
Skeletons and monsters, too.
But they don't frighten me, you see—
'Cause underneath, they're kids like me!

—Pamela Chanko

The Floppy Scarecrow

(Sing to the tune of "The Hokey Pokey")

You flop your right arm in, you flop your right arm out.
You flop your right arm in, and you shake it all about.
You do the Floppy Scarecrow, and the birds all fly around.
That's what it's all about!

You flop your left arm in, you flop your left arm out.
You flop your left arm in, and you shake it all about.
You do the Floppy Scarecrow, and the birds all fly around.
That's what it's all about.

You flop your right leg in, you flop your right leg out.
You flop your right leg in, and you shake it all about.
You do the Floppy Scarecrow, and the birds all fly around.
That's what it's all about.

You flop your left leg in, you flop your left leg out.
You flop your left leg in, and you shake it all about.
You do the Floppy Scarecrow, and the birds all fly around.
That's what it's all about.

—Pamela Chanko

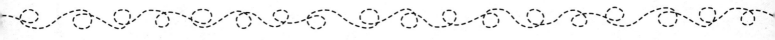

Thanksgiving

The year has turned its circle.
The seasons come and go.
The harvest is all gathered in,
And chilly north winds blow.

Orchards have shared their treasures,
The fields, their yellow grain,
So open wide the doorway,
Thanksgiving comes again!

       —Author Unknown

Help on Thanksgiving

I'm a holiday helper,
And I help with many things.
I help set the table,
Putting napkins in their rings.
I help do the dishes—
I can wash, and I can dry.
I help roll out the crust
To make a yummy pumpkin pie.
I help mash potatoes,
And I help stir the stew.
I help a lot with dinner—
And I help eat it, too!

       —Pamela Chanko

December Celebrations

Every year at just this time,
In cold and dark December,
Families around the world
All gather to remember,
With presents and with parties,
With feasting and with fun,
Customs and traditions
For people old and young.
So every year, around the world,
In all lands and nations,
People of all ages love
December celebrations!

       —Helen H. Moore

Happy Holidays

The holiday spirit is in the air,
And holiday lights are everywhere,
Menorahs, or kinaras,
Or Christmas lights that shimmer,
Everyone loves holidays, when
Stars and snowflakes glimmer.

—Helen H. Moore

Five Little Stockings

Five little stockings, hanging in a row,
Then a wind began to blow!
One fell down, now do you know
How many stockings are hanging in a row?

—Pamela Chanko

Tip: Create math word problems by changing the numbers in lines 1 and 3.

A Visit From St. Nicholas

'Twas the night before Christmas, when all through the house
Not a creature was stirring, not even a mouse.
The stockings were hung by the chimney with care,
In hopes that St. Nicholas soon would be there.
The children were nestled all snug in their beds,
While visions of sugar-plums danced in their heads.
And mamma in her 'kerchief, and I in my cap,
Had just settled our brains for a long winter's nap,
When out on the lawn there arose such a clatter,
I sprang from the bed to see what was the matter.
Away to the window I flew like a flash,
Tore open the shutters and threw up the sash.
The moon on the breast of the new-fallen snow
Gave the lustre of mid-day to objects below,
When, what to my wondering eyes should appear,
But a miniature sleigh, and eight tiny reindeer,
With a little old driver, so lively and quick,

I knew in a moment it must be St. Nick.
More rapid than eagles his coursers they came,
And he whistled, and shouted, and called them by name:
"Now, Dasher! now, Dancer! now, Prancer and Vixen!
On, Comet! on, Cupid! on, Donner and Blitzen!
To the top of the porch! to the top of the wall!
Now dash away! dash away! dash away all!"
As dry leaves that before the wild hurricane fly,
When they meet with an obstacle, mount to the sky,
So up to the house-top the coursers they flew,
With the sleigh full of toys, and St. Nicholas too.
And then, in a twinkling, I heard on the roof
The prancing and pawing of each little hoof.
As I drew in my head, and was turning around,
Down the chimney St. Nicholas came with a bound.
He was dressed all in fur, from his head to his foot,
And his clothes were all tarnished with ashes and soot;
A bundle of Toys he had flung on his back,
And he looked like a peddler just opening his pack.
His eyes—how they twinkled! his dimples how merry!
His cheeks were like roses, his nose like a cherry!
His droll little mouth was drawn up like a bow
And the beard of his chin was as white as the snow;
The stump of a pipe he held tight in his teeth,
And the smoke it encircled his head like a wreath;
He had a broad face and a little round belly,
That shook when he laughed, like a bowlful of jelly!
He was chubby and plump, a right jolly old elf,
And I laughed when I saw him, in spite of myself.
A wink of his eye and a twist of his head,
Soon gave me to know I had nothing to dread.
He spoke not a word, but went straight to his work,
And filled all the stockings; then turned with a jerk,
And laying his finger aside of his nose,
And giving a nod, up the chimney he rose.
He sprang to his sleigh, to his team gave a whistle,
And away they all flew like the down of a thistle.
But I heard him exclaim, ere he drove out of sight,
"Happy Christmas to all, and to all a good-night!"

—Clement Clark Moore

The Twenty-Fourth of December

The clock ticks slowly, slowly in the hall
And slower and more slowly the long hours crawl.
It seems as though today,
Would never pass away,
The clock ticks slowly, s-l-o-w-l-y in the hall.

—Author Unknown

Hanukkah Time

Light the Menorah!
Let's dance the hora!
Hanukkah is here!

Spin the dreidel,
Set the table,
Hanukkah is here!

—Helen H. Moore

Kwanzaa

"Habari gani"—what's the news?
What's the great occasion?
Let's pull together—"Harambee!"
To make a celebration.
It's Kwanzaa!
Time for unity,
And self-determination!
We'll share responsibility,
And show cooperation.
It's Kwanzaa!
Time for purpose,
Time for creativity,
And Kwanzaa's also time for faith.
It's Kwanzaa! Harambee!

—Helen H. Moore

New Year's Day

I have a birthday,
And so does each year,
On January first,
That day is here.

We say goodbye
To the year that is past.
We say hello
To the New Year at last!

—Helen H. Moore

Hello, New Year

Hello, New Year. Hello, New Year.
Here's to you! Here's to you!
(insert outgoing year) is over,
(insert incoming year) is now,
Out with the old and in with the new!

—Pamela Chanko

Chinese New Year

"Gung Hay Fat Choy!"
In China, every girl and boy
Celebrates the New Year
In a very special way—
With fireworks and dragons,
Colored red and gold,
They welcome in the New Year,
And chase away the old!

—Helen H. Moore

What's a President?

Our president
Is the resident
Of the White House, USA.

He works hard for our country
Each and every single day.

He keeps us safe and free and strong,
In this great world where we belong,

And we can see,
It's great to be,
The president of you and me!

—Helen H. Moore

George Washington

Everybody knows the story of the
cherry tree—
His father asked, "Who cut this
down?"
And young George answered, "Me!"
Now that's a pretty story, but
Between just me and you,
I don't think George would like it,
'cause
It's probably not true!
There are a lot of other things George
Washington DID do—
Like making maps, and farming, and
he was a soldier, too!
He was our country's president, the
very first we had.
But what do we remember? That old
tree of George's dad!

—Helen H. Moore

Mr. Lincoln

You know Mr. Lincoln—
No fancy clothes for him:
A stovepipe hat, a wrinkled coat,
And whiskers on his chin.

You know Mr. Lincoln,
His face is on the penny.
In life, that face was lined with care,
For troubles, he had many.

That brave Mr. Lincoln
Said slavery was wrong.
He led us through the Civil War
And kept our country strong.

That humble Mr. Lincoln
Had in him something grand
That helped him rise from poverty
To lead our mighty land.

—Helen H. Moore

What Is a Vote?

A vote means that
You get a say
In how we run the USA!
In how we work
And how we play,
In what we do
And say each day.

       —Helen H. Moore

Happy Birthday, MLK!

MLK was the son of a preacher.
His voice made freedom ring.
He was a leader and a teacher.

He spoke about peace,
About law, and fair play,
And so we honor MLK
On his special day.

       —Helen H. Moore

Martin Luther King, Jr.

When Martin was a little boy,
It made him sad and lonely
To see the parks and pools and schools
With signs that said "White Only."

He knew he had to change the world,
But had to do it right;
And that meant working peacefully—
No fists would win this fight.

So Martin grew and studied, too.
And came to speak his mind.
He led a march for equal rights
For all of humankind.

Dr. King did change the world,
As hard as that may seem;
But with an open mind and heart
You, too, can live his dream.

       —Pamela Chanko

Valentine's Day

On Valentine's Day
We show we care
For friends and family
Everywhere.

We send them cards
And sometimes candy.
Valentine's Day
Is really dandy.

—Helen H. Moore

Making a Valentine

I'm cutting out a great big heart.
I'm squeezing on some glue.
I'm writing out a message—
It's a valentine for you!
My valentine has words to read
And fuzzy felt to feel.
"I love you," says my valentine,
but words can't say how much!

—Pamela Chanko

Groundhog Day

When winter's frosty breath is all around,
And the groundhog doesn't see its shadow
On the cold, hard, winter ground,
Then it won't be long 'til springtime will be coming round!

—Helen H. Moore

Wake Up, Groundhog

Group 1:   Groundhog, groundhog, underground.
You slept all winter, safe and sound.

Group 2:   It's Groundhog Day! We're here to shout:
Wake up! Wake up! Now please come out!

Groundhog: Shhh, I'm sleeping. Can't you see?
Now go away and let me be!

Group 1:   Groundhog, groundhog, we must know!
Will we have six more weeks of snow?

Group 2:   Will you see your shadow today?
Or is warm weather on the way?

Ending A:

Groundhog: You woke me up! What's this I see?
My shadow, right in front of me!

Groups 1 & 2:   Six weeks of winter are ahead!

Groundhog: So I am going back to bed!

Ending B:

Groundhog: You woke me up? What's this I see?
No shadow is in front of me!

Groups 1 & 2:   Spring's almost here, you sleepyhead!

Groundhog: I'm glad you got me out of bed!

—Pamela Chanko

One Hundredth Day of School

One hundred days of learning,
One hundred days of fun.
One hundred ways to grow and play,
To read, and write, and run.
To see our teachers and our friends,
To eat at lunchtime, too.
One hundred ways,
One hundred days,
Of school for me and you!

—Helen H. Moore

Women's History Month

Why do they call it "his-story?"
It's really quite a mystery!
It should be "hers-and-history"
If you ask me!
'Cause women like Harriet Tubman
helped people to be free!
And women got to vote with help from
Susan B. Anthony!
So history was made by hims and hers, you see...
In this land of equal opportunity!

—Helen H. Moore

Shamrock Rock

Let's do the
Shamrock rock.
Let's do the
Shamrock roll.
We've got the shamrock feeling
Way down in our soul.
We've got a St. Paddy's rainbow
And a pot of gold,
And the St. Paddy's feeling
Down in our soul!

—Helen H. Moore

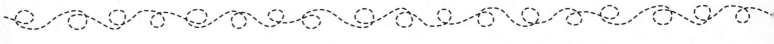

St. Patrick's Day Is Almost Here

When shamrocks are showing
All over town,
St. Patrick's Day
Must be coming around.
Yes,
March seventeen
Is the day to be seen.
It's the day when we just have to wear
Something green!

—Helen H. Moore

Earth Day Lesson

Chief Seattle was a teacher
Who taught us how to care
For all the living things on earth,
Fresh water, and clean air.
"The earth does not belong to us,"
Great Chief Seattle said.
"We sometime think it does, but
we belong to the earth, instead."

—Helen H. Moore

Easter

Easter baskets,
Easter treats,
Easter clothes, and
Easter sweets.

When Easter comes,
The birds all sing,
They know that Easter
Means it's spring!

—Helen H. Moore

Flag Day

I am the flag, I fly.
I tell the world a story
About our country's birth
About our nation's glory.

Thirteen stripes of red and white
And fifty stars on blue,
I tell the world I'm proud to be
American, aren't you?

—Helen H. Moore

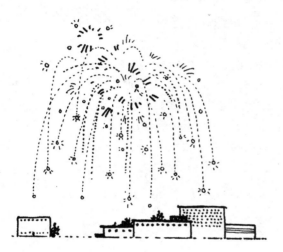

Independence Day

Let's have a parade!
Let's drink lemonade!
Let's have a picnic
In the shade!

Let's celebrate
This happy day,
When we became
The USA!

—Helen H. Moore

Labor Day

When I grow up,
I'll go to work,
Just like the grown-ups do.
On Labor Day,
I'll get to say,
That I'm a worker, too!

—Helen H. Moore

Whatever the Weather

Rainbow Paintbox

I can see a rainbow, see it in the sky,
See it when the rain has gone away.

Colors of the rainbow,
In the sky so high,

I can name them all for you today:
Red there is, a rosy red, a red so bright and bonny,

And orange as a tiger lily leaf so bold and tawny,
Yellow as the blazing sun that gives us all our light,

And green as grass beneath our feet,
Blue as the sky so bright,

There's indigo, as dark as night,
And violet like flowers.

These are the colors nature paints
The sky with after showers.

—Christina G. Rossetti

The Rain

The rain is raining all around;
It falls on field and tree,
It rains on the umbrellas here,
And on the ships at sea.

—Robert Louis Stevenson

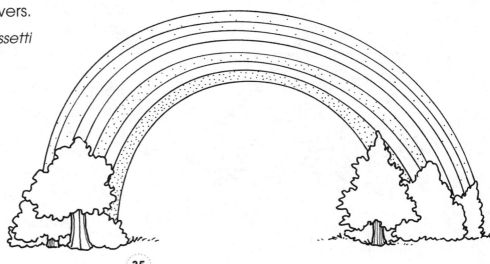

Raindrops

rain
drops
drip
down
all
day
long

drip down
slip down
splashing out their song.

thunder-crashing
splashing
splashing
slipping
dripping

raining down
their rain
raindrop
song

—Helen H. Moore

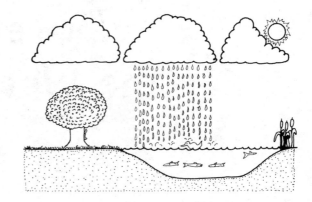

The Water Cycle

When I was young
I used to think
that water came from
the kitchen sink.

But now I'm older,
and I know,
that water comes
from rain and snow.
It stays there, waiting,
in the sky,
in clouds above
our world so high.
And when it falls,
it flows along,
and splashes out
a watery song,
as each raindrop
is joined by more
and rushes
to the ocean shore,
or to a lake, a brook, a stream,
from which it rises,
Just like steam.
but while it's down here
what do you think?
Some DOES go to
the kitchen sink!

—Helen H. Moore

Storm

Outside, thunder crashes!
Outside, lightning flashes!
Outside, wild rain lashes!

Inside, we are safe.
Inside, we are warm.
Inside, there is comfort.
Outside, there is STORM!

—Helen H. Moore

Snow Day

Snow day,
Snow day,
Get up and go day!
See the wind blow day!
Go with the flow day!
Wonderful, wonderful, wonderful
Snow day!

—Helen H. Moore

Snow Words

Snow jacket, snow boots
Snow pants, snow suits.
Snowflakes, snowstorm—
Snow is cold, but we feel warm!

—Helen H. Moore

Snow Surprise!

I woke up this morning, and
What do you know?
I went to the window,
And looked down below.
I saw that the world
Was all covered with snow!
Will we go to school today?
I don't think so,
'Cause when it's a snow day,
We don't get to go!

—Helen H. Moore

Snowman

Snowflakes falling
thick and fast
build a snowman
make him last…

Snowflakes falling
swirling, slow,
my snowman melted—
where'd he go?

—Helen H. Moore

Who Has Seen the Wind?

Who has seen the wind?
Neither I nor you:
But when the leaves hang trembling
The wind is passing through.

Who has seen the wind?
Neither you nor I:
But when the trees bow down their heads
The wind is passing by.

—Christina G. Rossetti

One Windy Day

*(Note: Fill in the blanks
with any item you like.)*

I was playing outside
One fine summer day,
When whoosh! A big wind
Took my _____ away!

But when it died down,
It was calm as could be—
And that kind of little breeze
Gave my _____ back to me!

—Pamela Chanko

The Leaves

The leaves had a wonderful frolic.
They danced to the wind's loud song.
They whirled, and they floated and
scampered.
They circled and flew along.

The moon saw the little leaves dancing.
Each looked like a small brown bird.
The man in the moon smiled and listened,
And this is the song he heard.

The North Wind is calling, is calling.
And we must whirl round and round.
And then, when our dance has ended,
We'll make a warm quilt on the ground.

—Author Unknown

A Kite

I often sit and wish that I
Could be a kite up in the sky,
And ride upon the wind and go,
Whichever way I chanced to blow.

—*Author Unknown*

Seeing Things

I lie
On my back
In the green and fragrant grass,
And I gaze
At the clouds
In the sky.

And to me
What I see
Looks like a menagerie
As in the green and fragrant grass
I lie.

I see
Turtles in a pool.
Lots of fishes in a school,
And a lizard who is quite a cutie-pie!

I see kittens in a box,
And a rabbit, wearing socks,
As I watch the clouds above
Float by!

—*Helen H. Moore*

Shadow

Do you see my shadow?
It goes where I go,
It does the things that I do
Never too quickly, never too slow.

My shadow's dark, when the day is bright,
And then it disappears at night.
Does it rest, I wonder,
When I'm sleeping, tucked up tight?

— *Helen H. Moore*

Hot Weather

It's hot!
So what?
I like it that way.
I love a hot day,
When I can just play,
When I can eat ice cream,
And splash in the street,
Or get cool in the pool,
That's a hot-weather treat!

— *Helen H. Moore*

Best Me I Can Be!

Best Me I Can Be!

I always try to be the best,
Don't want to be the worst,

But there are times I come in last
When I want to come in first.

I want to be the Number One,
Not Number Two or Three,

But one prize I always win—
I'm the Best Me I Can Be!

—Helen H. Moore

Please

Do you know
There's a magic word
That makes things happen?
Haven't you heard?

Please is the word.
With a magic way, it
Makes things happen—
You just have to say it—
Please!

—Helen H. Moore

My Feelings and Me

I cry when I am very sad.
I stomp my foot when I am mad.
Excitement sometimes makes me jump.
When I feel bad, my shoulders slump.
Sometimes I feel very shy,
But then I laugh and don't know why!
I show my feelings, 'cause you see,
My feelings are a part of me!

—Pamela Chanko

Thank You

When I remember
To say "thank you,"
I'm telling you I really like
The nice things that you do.

—Helen H. Moore

Thank you.

I Can Share

If I had a yummy treat,
I would give you some to eat.
And if I had a brand new book,
I would let you come and look.
And if you had some work to do,
I'd help you out and share that, too.
And if I had a whole free day,
We'd share it and we'd laugh and play.

—Pamela Chanko

Cooperation

We work together,
To get a job done.
Working together
Makes work fun!

Together, together,
That's the way,
Cooperate,
At work or play.

—Helen H. Moore

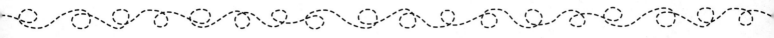

The Fight

I have a friend.
We had a fight.
I cried myself
To sleep last night.

And when I see
My friend today,
I'll say, "I'm sorry.
Want to play?"

I hope she'll say
She's sorry, too.
I'm sure she will—
That's what friends do.

        —*Helen H. Moore*

Grow Food

Grow food,
Grow food,
It's get-up-and-go food—
Grow food is food
That is healthy to eat,
That helps us grow strong
From our heads to our feet.
Grow food is vegetables,
Eggs, milk, and meat,
And fruit when we've just gotta have
Something sweet!

        —*Helen H. Moore*

Exercise Is Fun

Jump and stretch,
Get into the groove,
If you want a healthy body,
You've got to move!

Arms and legs
And hips and knees,
Wiggle those
And wriggle these!

Jump and stretch,
Get into the groove,
If you want a healthy body,
You've got to move!

        —*Helen H. Moore*

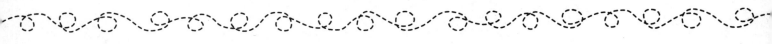

If You're Healthy and You Know It

(Sing to the tune of
"If You're Happy and You Know It")

If you're healthy and you know it,
Brush your teeth. Brush, brush!
If you're healthy and you know it,
Brush your teeth. Brush, brush!
If you're healthy and you know it,
And you really want to show it,
If you're healthy and you know it,
Brush your teeth. Brush, brush!

If you're healthy and you know it,
Wash your hands. Wash, wash!
If you're healthy and you know it,
Wash your hands. Wash, wash!
If you're healthy and you know it,
And you really want to show it,
If you're healthy and you know it,
Wash your hands. Wash, wash!

If you're healthy and you know it,
Get your rest. Zzzz, zzzz!
If you're healthy and you know it,
Get your rest. Zzzz, zzzz!
If you're healthy and you know it,
And you really want to show it,
If you're healthy and you know it,
Get your rest. Zzzz, zzzz!

—*Pamela Chanko*

My Super Senses

My nose is there to help me smell.
My ears can help me hear a bell.
My fingers help me touch and feel.
My mouth can taste a yummy meal.
My eyes are there to look about.
My senses help me find things out.

—Pamela Chanko

Good Food

Food has to come from somewhere
Before it's on our table.
Think about the foods you eat
And see if you are able
To tell where each one comes from,
From field or farm or tree.
Because food comes from somewhere
Before it gets to you and me.

An apple comes from an apple tree.
A fish comes from the deep, blue sea.
The slice of bread you like to eat
Came from a field of golden wheat.
A glass of water, clear and plain,
Got started as a drop of rain.
Think about the foods you eat,
Each time you have a tasty treat.
Try new foods, and don't say "no,"
Eat good food that helps you grow.

—Helen H. Moore

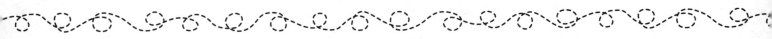

Tooth Truth

I have a little space
In the middle of my face,

And in that space
there used to be a tooth.

It was little,
it was white,

And it just fell out one night,
And a fairy came and took it,
That's the truth!

The fairy gave me money
When she took my tooth away,
Took it from the pillow it was under.
But what do fairies want with teeth
That they get from underneath
My pillow as I'm sleeping,
That, I wonder.

—Helen H. Moore

I Am Sick

My stuffy nose,
Is as red as a rose.

I'm achy and hot
From my head to my toes!

—Helen H. Moore

Swinging

Hold on tight,
Bend your knees,
Lean far back,
Feel the breeze.
Pump that swing,
Feel it go,
Swing up high,
Swoop down low,
And SWING!

—Helen H. Moore

Family, Friends, Community

Family

If your father
or your mother
has a sister
or a brother
Then you've got an aunt or uncle,
Or an uncle or an aunt!

Now if your mother's brother
Has some children of his own,
And if your daddy's sister
Has some half- or fully grown,
Then you've got yourself some cousins,
(You might have 'em by the dozens!)

—Helen H. Moore

Dozens of Cousins

You might have a cousin Claude,
You might have a cousin Maude,
Or an Amy
Or a Jenny
Or a Burton
Or a Benny
Or an Ethan
Or a Leo
Or a Scarlet
Or a Theo
Or a Damien
Or a Dash
Or a Clementine
Or a Nash
Or a Collin
Or a Rose
That's the way a family grows!
With dozens of cousins,
Or even a few,
You'll have lots of people
Related to you!

—Helen H. Moore

You Are You, I Am Me

(Sing to the tune of "This Old Man")

You are you.
I am me.
We are different,
Can't you see?
Different eyes,
Different hair,
Different voices to sing song—
But we can all get along!

I'm like you.
You're like me,
We're alike,
Oh, can't you see?
Every place,
Far and wide,
Kids are just like me and you—
That's because they're children, too!

—Pamela Chanko

We Are One World

Pierre lives in Canada,
Maria lives in Spain.
But both like to ride their bikes
Along a shady lane.

Liv lives in Norway,
Ramon is in Peru.
But both laugh with the giraffe
When visiting the zoo.

Anwar is Egyptian.
Kim is Japanese.
But both run beneath the sun
And fly kites in the breeze.

Jack is from the USA,
Karintha is from Chad.
But both can write a poem at night
Upon a writing pad.

Children live all over,
The world's a giant ball.
But far and near, it's very clear
We're one world after all.

—Meish Goldish

Neighbors

I have some neighbors,
One, two, three,
They live on either
Side of me.

We help each other,
One, two, three,
And that's called being
Neighborly!

—Helen H. Moore

City and Country

Sometimes we go to the city,
And some people call it the town.
The people are all in a hurry there,
And they never seem to slow down.

Sometimes we go to the country,
Where the flowers and fields grow so lush,
Where animals play in the sunshine all day,
And there isn't so much of a rush.

—Helen H. Moore

Homes

My house is my home,
It's the place where I stay.
I go there to sleep
At the end of each day,
Where my family gathers
To eat, work, and play,
Wherever you live is your home!

Your home can be big,
Or your home can be small.
In a street lined with trees,
Or a skyscraper, tall,
Your home is the place that
You love most of all,
Your wonderful, beautiful home!

—Helen H. Moore

The Wheels on the Bus

The wheels on the bus go round and round,
Round and round, round and round.
The wheels on the bus go round and round,
All through the town.

The driver on the bus says, "Step to the rear!
Step to the rear! Step to the rear!"
The driver on the bus says, "Step to the rear!"
All through the town.

The people on the bus go up and down,
Up and down, up and down.
The people on the bus go up and down,
All through the town.

The kids on the bus go yakkity-yack,
Yakkity-yak, yakkity-yak.
The kids on the bus go yakkity-yack,
All through the town.

The driver on the bus says, "Quiet, please!
Quiet, please! Quiet, please!"
The driver on the bus says, "Quiet, please!"
All through the town.

The wheels on the bus go round and round,
Round and round, round and round.
The wheels on the bus go round and round,
All through the town.

—Author Unknown

Airplane

The airplane taxis down the field
And heads into the breeze.
It lifts its wheels above the ground.
It skims above the trees.
It rises high and higher
Away up toward the sun.
It's just a speck against the sky
And now—
And now—it's gone!

—Author Unknown

Transportation

Ships sail over water.
Planes fly through the air.
Cars and trains roll over land,
And take us everywhere!

—Helen H. Moore

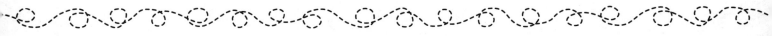

The Colors of Safety

You know that red means stop, stop, stop,
And green means go, go, go,
But when the light turns yellow
It means Please Go Very Slow!

—*Helen H. Moore*

Community Helpers

The crossing guard
Helps keep us safe
As we walk across the street.

The trash collector's job
Helps keep our
Sidewalks clean and neat.

The officer who drives around
Is sometimes called a cop.
She watches our community,
In a car with lights on top.

—*Helen H. Moore*

The Mail Carrier

See the mail carrier, swinging along.
Her bag is deep and wide.
And messages from all over the world
Are bundled up inside.

—*Author Unknown*

Police Officer

Officer, Officer,
Help me please.
I'm a little bit lost,
And I'm starting to sneeze!
If I can't get back home,
I'm afraid I will freeze!
Oh, Officer, help me, please!

Officer, Officer,
Thanks a bunch.
You brought me home
In time for lunch,
And now I can have
Some lunch to munch.
So Officer, thanks
A bunch!

—Helen H. Moore

Brave Firefighters

(Sing to the tune of "I'm a Little Teapot")

They are brave firefighters, there's no doubt.
If there's a fire, give them a shout.
Their fire engine takes the fastest route,
Then they'll work until that fire's out.

—Pamela Chanko

Doctor

I'd like to be a doctor,
Helping people who are sick.
I'd like to wear a stethoscope
So I could hear hearts tick.

I'd like to be a doctor,
Because I'd like to know
the way the human body works,
and what it needs to grow.

—Helen H. Moore

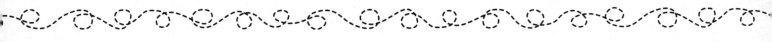

The Recycling Dance

(Sing to the tune of "The Hokey Pokey")

You put the plastic in,
You leave the garbage out,
You put the plastic in,
And then something new comes out!
Recycle and you'll help your town,
As the Earth spins 'round and 'round.
That's what it's all about!

—*Pamela Chanko*

Mystery Mouse

There's a mouse,
In my house,
But it's not the kind you think.

It doesn't nibble cookies
And it doesn't need a drink.

It rolls around its mouse pad,
Like it is on a scooter,
I bet you guessed, my special pet
Is part of my computer!

—*Helen H. Moore*

How We Move

People and animals
Move and go.
Some move fast,
Some move slow.

Penguins waddle,
Toddlers toddle,
Panthers pace,
All over the place.
Gorillas bump,
And swing, and jump,
And pound their chests
With a mighty thump!

Moving fast,
Moving slow,
People and animals,
Go, go, go!

—*Helen H. Moore*

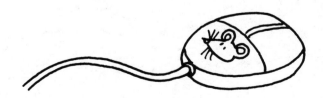

Letter Learning

Alphabet Cheer

A is for awesome,
B is for busy.
C is for careful,
D is for dizzy!

E is for excellent,
F is for flappy.
G is for grumpy,
H is for happy!

I is for interesting,
J is for jumpy.
K is for kind,
L is for lumpy!

M is for magical,
N is for nice.
O is for orange,
P's for precise.

Q is for quiet,
R is for rusty.
S is for special,
T is for trusty.

U's for unusual,
V is for vexed.
W's for wild,
X is for x'ed!

Y is for yellow,
Z is for zany.
I know all my letters—
Which means I am brainy.

—Pamela Chanko

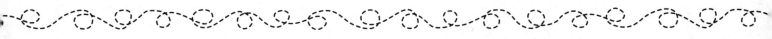

Hooray for A! (A)

A is for apple
And also for ape.
An ape can eat an apple and
An ape can wear a cape!

—Helen H. Moore

The Best of B (B)

B is for best,
B is for better,
B is for a big bear in a blue sweater!

—Helen H. Moore

Deer Dash (D)

Dogs dig,
Dolphins splash,
Ducklings paddle,
Deer dash!

—Helen H. Moore

Cats Creep (C)

Cats creep,
Cows moo,
Crows cackle,
Crocodiles chew!

—Helen H. Moore

Excellent "E" (E)

E is excellent,
E is easy,
E is very sweet.
Can you find two little e's
In the middle of your feet?

—Helen H. Moore

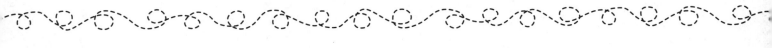

Finch Feathers (F)

Far, far off the ground,
Flies a feathery fellow.
He's a fine-looking finch,
With a body so round
And feathers fine and yellow.

—Helen H. Moore

Gooey, Gooey Gumbo! (G)

Gooey, gooey gumbo!
Gooey, gooey gumbo!
Make mine jumbo—
'Cause I love gooey gumbo!

—Helen H. Moore

Hanna the Hungry Hippo (H)

Hanna was a hippo.
Hanna ate some honey.
Hanna got the hiccups,
And it really wasn't funny!

A hippo with the hiccups
Isn't happy, she is sore.
Hungry Hanna hippo
Won't eat honey anymore.

—Helen H. Moore

I Love Ice Cream (I)

I love ice cream!
I love pie!
I love ocean!
I love sky!
I love iguanas and insects, too!
But not as much as I love you!

—Megan Duhamel

Jelly Jiggles (J)

Jelly jiggles.
Jam is sweet.
Both of them
Are fun to eat.

Jam is sticky.
Jelly is, too,
Sticky and icky,
Just like glue!

You will be sticky
if you get some on you!

—*Helen H. Moore*

Look and Listen (L)

Look, look, look,
At the letters in my book.

Listen to me when I read,
Words and letters, yes indeed.

Look and listen, listen and look,
at lovely me, with my lovely book.

—*Helen H. Moore*

Kangaroo Pocket (K)

Kangaroo, oh Kangaroo,
I'd like to have a pocket,
Like you do.

I'd keep my baby
Kangaroo,
Inside my pocket,
Just like you!

I'd kiss my baby Kangaroo.
We'd go to karaoke,
We'd sing and dance and jump around
And do the hokey-pokey!

—*Helen H. Moore*

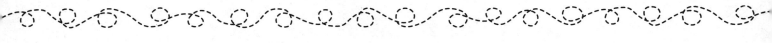

Mmmmmmm! (M)

Mmmmmmm! Mmmmmmm!
Mmmmmmm!
The letter M
Is yummy!
That's the sound I make when
something good
Is in my tummy!

Mmmmmmm! Mmmmmmm!
Mmmmmmm!
Mangos, macaroni,
Muffins, milk, and meat!
Foods that begin with the letter M
Are oh so good to eat!

—*Helen H. Moore*

Nice and Naughty (N)

N can be naughty,
N can be nice.
N is in *never*,
But never in mice!

—*Helen H. Moore*

Oh, No (O)

Oh, no!
It's time to go!
I want you to know
That when I say "Oh, no,"
It's 'cause I want to stay with you,
I just don't want to go!

—*Helen H. Moore*

Puppies Peek (P)

Puppies peek,
Ponies prance,
Piglets squeak,
Penguins dance!

—*Helen H. Moore*

The Question of Q (Q)

Q must be shy.
Q is never alone.
Q needs a U
So he's not on his own.

In words like *quiet*,
And *question*,
And *quilt*, you see they go together.
Q always sticks with U
In any kind of weather!

—*Helen H. Moore*

Sassy Snakes (S)

Skunks have stripes
Down the middle of their back.
Snails crawl around and
Leave sticky tracks.
Sleek seals like to splash and play
And sassy snakes say "SSSSSSSSSSS" all day!

—*Helen H. Moore*

Rabbits Race (R)

Rabbits race
Rivers run,
And roosters wake up
Everyone!

—*Helen H. Moore*

T-rrific Critters (T)

Toads hop,
Turkeys gobble,
Tigers growl,
Turtles wobble!

Trout swim,
Tadpoles wiggle.
T-rrific creatures
Make me giggle!

—*Helen H. Moore*

Wonderful U (U)

Are you up in the air?
Or
Are you under there?
"U" are the one I seek—
You're so utterly unique!

—Helen H. Moore

A Van Can (V)

A van can carry vegetables.
A van can carry vases.
A van can carry valentines
That come from far-off places.

A van can carry vampire bats
Or very, very friendly rats,
Or even fancy velvet hats
Made in Vermont for spoiled cats.

—Helen H. Moore

Wow, It's W! (W)

I want to say a word
About a wow of a letter.
You use it in the winter
When you wear a woolly sweater.
You can see it in Hawaii,
You can write it on a wall.
Can you guess what that letter is?
It's W, after all!

—Helen H. Moore

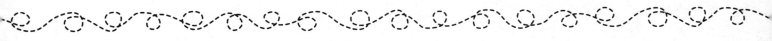

An Example of X (X)

X is for X-rays
That show your insides.
X-rays show things
Your skin usually hides.

—*Helen H. Moore*

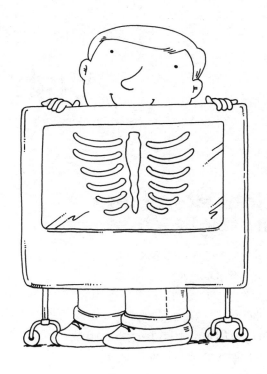

Yawning Yak (Y)

A yawning yak
Lay on his back,
Waiting for me to bake.
Now that yawning yak
Went and stuffed his sack
With my yummy yellow cake!

—*Helen H. Moore*

Zelda the Zebra (Z)

Zelda the zebra loves zany clothes.
She loves to prance. She loves to pose.
She zooms 'round the zoo in fuzzy slippers
And fancy pants with a zillion zippers!

—*Megan Duhamel*

Super Sight Words

Sight Words Are the Right Words

Sight words are words
You've just got to know.
You can't sound them out
Even if you go slow.
You just have to learn them
And when you do, say:
"I know all my sight words—
Hip, hip, hip, hooray!"

—*Helen H. Moore*

And, And, And (and)

The pigs are in the mud
And the cows are in the barn
And the horses are in the big corral
And they all live on the farm!

—*Helen H. Moore*

I Had a Hen (a)

I had a hen,
She laid one egg,
And then she laid another.

Two fluffy chicks
Came from those eggs,
A sister and a brother.

—*Helen H. Moore*

As Floppy as a Noodle (as)

As floppy as a noodle,
As yappy as a poodle,
As sunny as a summer day,
As happy as a child at play,
As big as a bear, tall as a tree,
Or as small as small as small can be.

— Helen H. Moore

Wish Away (away)

Far away,
Far away,
Over the hills
And far away
Is where I wish
To go someday.

I wish I could
I wish I may,
Go over the hills
And far away.

— Helen H. Moore

Big Animals (big)

Big bear,
Big hippo,
Big elephant, too.
But none can compare
To the big, big, whale,
Who can't even fit in the zoo!

— Megan Duhamel

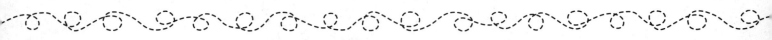

Blue Is a Berry (blue)

Blue is a butterfly
in the warm breeze,
flying so high
above rainforest trees.

Blue is a berry
so round and so sweet,
bursting with juice,
it's my favorite treat.

Blue is the ocean
and blue is the sky,
blue can be the color
of somebody's eye.
How many blue things
can you spy?

—Helen H. Moore

I Can Read (can)

I can tell daddy,
I can tell mother,
I can tell sister,
I can tell brother.
I can tell my kitten
and the goldfish, too:

I can read!
I can read!
I can read!
How 'bout you?

—Megan Duhamel

Come and Play (come)

Please come and play
With me today.
I cannot wait!
You know the way!
You can come with your cat,
You can come with your dog,
You can come with your snake
Or your little green frog!
Come in September!
Come in May!
Just come on over
And play, play, play!

—Helen H. Moore

Down, Down, Down (down)

A red leaf fell
Down, down, down.
A yellow leaf fell
Down, down, down.
An orange leaf fell
Down, down, down,
A brown leaf fell,
Down, down, down.
What's on the ground all over town?
The crisp fall leaves that fell
Down, down, down!

—Megan Duhamel

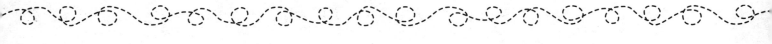

Never Ever (ever)

Did you ever?
No, I never?
That was clever!
Was it ever!
I could keep this up forever!

     —Helen H. Moore

Find a Button (find)

Find a button,
Find a penny,
Find a piece of candy,
Open up your eyes and look—
You may find something dandy.

     —Helen H. Moore

Just for Fun (for)

I bounced my ball
Against a wall,
I did it just for fun,
I rode my bike,
The bike I like,
I did it just for fun.
I climbed a tree,
High as can be,
I did it just for fun.
So many things I do because
They're lots of fun, you see!

     —Helen H. Moore

Look What I Found! (found)

Look what I found!
Look what I found!
I found a shiny penny
Right there on the ground!

     —Helen H. Moore

Funny Bunny (funny)

Funny bunny,
Hopping all about,
You jump into that jolly basket,
Then you jump back out!

—Helen H. Moore

Go! Go! Go! (go)

We have a little brother,
And we take him where we go.
We put him in his stroller,
And we push him fast and slow.
But when we push him too slow
He hollers, "Go! Go! Go!"
Our little brother likes it
When we take him where we go.

—Helen H. Moore

How I Grow (grow)

Shall I show
You what I know?

What I know
Is how to grow!

I eat and sleep and play and so—
I get to grow and grow and grow!

—Helen H. Moore

He (he)

My brother and I
Are twins, you see,
But I am not him,
And he is not me!
He is the short one
I am tall.
I like skating,
He plays ball,
But he is my brother,
I'm his, and that's all!

—Helen H. Moore

Here I Am (here)

Here I am,
Look at me,
Here I am up in a tree.
I've got wings and I fly free,
Here in my nest in the tall, tall tree!

—Helen H. Moore

We All Help (help)

I help my father and
My father helps my mother.
My mother helps my sister,
And my sister helps my brother.
And every day
We laugh and play
By helping one another!

—Helen H. Moore

I Am Me! (I)

I am me!
I am me!
I am me!
It's plain to see!

I am me!
I am me!
I am the only me
That will ever be!

—Megan Duhamel

Is It This or That? (is)

I wonder what this is?
I wonder what's that?
Is it a kitten?
Or is it a cat?
Is it a mitten?
Or is it a hat?
I wonder,
I wonder,
What's this?
And what's that?

—Helen H. Moore

Come In (in)

Come in, come in,
Come in from the storm.
Come in to my cozy house
And get toasty warm!

—Helen H. Moore

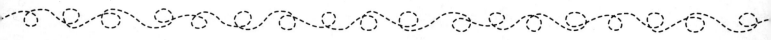

I Saw It, Too! (it)

Did you see that?
I saw it, too!
Was it a hat?
Or was it a shoe?
I couldn't tell,
I couldn't say,
But I know I saw it
Anyway!

—Helen H. Moore

If You Make a Promise (make)

If you make a promise
It's important not to break it.
If you plan to break it,
Then, it's better not to make it.
Better, better, better
Not to make it make it make it.

—Helen H. Moore

Me, Me, Me (me)

Me, me, me!
I like to sing.
Me, me, me!
I like to swing.
Me, me, me!
I like to share
With you, you, you—
My friend out there!

—Megan Duhamel

I Look in the Mirror (look)

I look in the mirror
And what do I see?
A pair of eyes
Looking back at me.

I look in the mirror
And what do I see?
I look in the mirror
And I see ME!

—Helen H. Moore

Not (not)

Was it new?
It was not.
Was it hot?
It was not.
Was it big?
It was not.
Did you like it?
Not a jot!
My, oh my, there are a lot
Of things that are not, not, not!

—Helen H. Moore

I Can Jump Over (over)

I can jump over
a sidewalk crack.
I can jump over
my toy train track.

I can jump over
a bumpy log.
I can jump over
a toad or a frog.

I can jump over
a stone or two.
But I can't jump over
that bird—it just flew!

—Jaime Lucero

Only One (one)

There is only one moon.
There is only one sky.
There is only one me.
There is only one I.

Only is special.
Only's such fun.
Only is wonderful.
Only's just one.

—Helen H. Moore

Play (play)

Play is fun,
Play is cool.
We play
When we come home from school.
We play inside,
And outdoors, too.
I really like to play,
Don't you?

—Helen H. Moore

My Pup Can Run (run)

My pup can run on four feet,
And I can run on two.
We run and play,
And have fun all day,
That's what we like to do.

—Helen H. Moore

I Love Red (red)

Red rocks, red socks,
Red wagons,
Red blocks,
Red rooster,
Red hen,
Name them all,
Then do it again,
'Cause I love red!

—Helen H. Moore

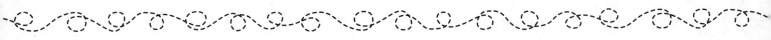

What the Animals Said (said)

"It's still dark,"
Said the lark.

"What's that?"
Said the cat.

"I want to sleep,"
Said the sheep.

"Of course,"
Said the horse.

"Let's have a spree,"
Said the bee.

"But where?"
Said the hare.

"In the barrow,"
Said the sparrow.

"I'm too big,"
Said the pig.

"In the house,"
Said the mouse.

But the dog said,
"Bow-wow. It's too late now!"
  —Author Unknown

See the Water (see)

See the water,
See the sky,
See the people
Passing by.

—Helen H. Moore

She Is Super (she)

She is super,
She is smart,
She is the one
Who has my heart.

—Helen H. Moore

Sleep Time (sleep)

I climb into bed
And I don't make a peep.
I pull up the covers
and sleep, sleep, sleep.

I sleep all night
And when I rise,
The bright sunshine
Tickles my eyes!

—Helen H. Moore

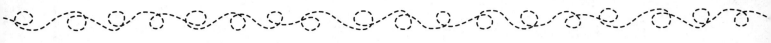

I'm Not Too Small (small)

I'm not too small,
I'm not too tall,
I'm big enough
To climb a wall.
I'm not too small,
To throw a ball,
In fact, I'm not too small at all!

—Helen H. Moore

The Moon (the)

The moon is lovely, big, and bright,
It shines up in the sky at night,
And lights the night with lovely light,
The moon is lovely, big, and bright.

—Helen H. Moore

Not Soon Enough (soon)

Soon is never soon enough
When something's on the way.
Soon is always much too long
For me to wait for, anyway!

—Helen H. Moore

Together We Can (together)

Together we can work.
Together we can play.
Together we can go.
Together we can stay.

We can work and we can play,
Come or go or stop or stay.
We can do things our own way,
When we stick together.

—Helen H. Moore

To the Fair (to)

I went to a party,
I went to the park,
I went to the fair,
and came home in the dark!

—Helen H. Moore

Three Little Cats (three)

Three cats
In three hats
Sat on three mats
Having three chats
Until three dogs told them to scat
And that was that was that.

—Megan Duhamel

Two Best Friends (two)

Me and you
We are two—
The two best friends in town!
Me and you
We are two—
The two best friends around!

—Helen H. Moore

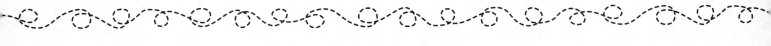

Up (up)

When I grow up, I want to be
Able to climb the tallest tree.
Up there in the branches,
I know I could see
Butterflies, birds, maybe even a bee!
When I grow up, I will see.

—Helen H. Moore

Well, Well, Well (well)

(Note: Build on the existing poem by substituting other animal sounds and animals.)

Ding-Dong-<u>Moo</u>!
Well, well, well,
I can tell
A <u>cow</u> is ringing
My doorbell.

Ding-Dong-<u>Baaah</u>!
Well, well, well,
I can tell
A <u>sheep</u> is ringing
My doorbell.

Ding-dong-<u>squeak</u>!
Well, well, well,
I can tell
A <u>mouse</u> is ringing
My doorbell.

Ding-dong-<u>neigh</u>!
Well, well, well,
I can tell
A <u>horse</u> is ringing
My doorbell.

Ding-dong-<u>cock-a-doodle-do</u>!
Well, well, well,
I can tell
A <u>rooster</u> is ringing
My doorbell.

—Helen H. Moore

We Are We (we)

He and she
And you and me
All together,
We're a WE!

We are not a YOU,
We are not a THEM,
We are not a HER,
We are not a HIM.

Oh, say, can you see
That we are a WE!

—Helen H. Moore

When I Wash (when)

When I wash,
My hands and face,
The soap goes slosh!
All over the place.

When I wash
My toes and feet,
The soap goes slosh!
Oh, what a treat!

When I wash me
I get so clean,
But I make the bath
A messy scene!

—Helen H. Moore

Which One? (which)

Which one do you want?
The pink or the blue?
Which one is for me?
Which one is for you?
Which hat should I wear?
Which toy should I share?
Which one would you like?
Or do you even care?

—Helen H. Moore

Yellow (yellow)

Yellow is a buttercup,
Yellow is some corn,
Yellow is a baby chick,
On a pretty summer morn.

—Helen H. Moore

You, You, You (you)

You, you, you,
And the things you can do.
You can brush your teeth,
You can tie your shoe,
You can go for a walk,
You can visit the zoo.
You can do all these things,
You, wonderful you!

—Helen H. Moore

Reading, Writing & 'Rithmetic

Reading

When I was little,
I could look
At the pictures
In my book,
But now I'm older,
Yes, indeed,
And I can read, and read, and read!

—*Helen H. Moore*

Books Are Good!

If you read a few,
then you'll know it's true:
Books are good for you!
Chefs read cookbooks,
Pirates read hook books,
Little kids read lift-and-look books!
We read books of poems and prose—
Some of these and some of those.
Read some too, and you'll agree,
Books are good for you and me!

—*Helen H. Moore*

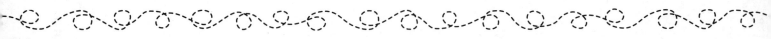

Author, Author

A plot is the part of a story
that tells you who did what,
Like Gretel and her brother
In the mean old witch's hut.

The characters in the story
Are the people it happens to,
Like Ariel the Mermaid,
Or even Scooby-Doo!

The author of the story
Writes it down for you.
A kid who likes to write
May someday be an author, too!

—Helen H. Moore

Spelling

When I am spelling,
I'm really just telling,
The letters in the words I know,
Just where they are supposed to go!

—Helen H. Moore

Noun, Verb, Adjective

A noun is the word for a thing,
Like a book, or a swing, or a ring.

Verbs are words about doing,
Like drinking and eating and
chewing.

Adjectives tell what kind of a thing
A noun is, like a broken swing,
Or a picture book, or a golden ring.

—Helen H. Moore

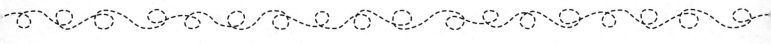

Parts of Speech

Three little words you often see
Are ARTICLES: *a, an,* and *the.*

A NOUN's the name of anything,
As: *school* or *garden, toy,* or *swing.*

ADJECTIVES tell the kind of noun,
As: *great, small, pretty, white,* or *brown.*

VERBS tell of something being done:
To *read, write, count, sing, jump,* or *run.*

How things are done the ADVERBS tell,
As: *slowly, quickly, badly, well.*

CONJUNCTIONS join the words together,
As: men *and* women, wind *or* weather.

The PREPOSITION stands before
A noun, as: *in* or *through* a door.

The INTERJECTION shows surprise,
As: *Oh,* how pretty! *Ah!* How wise!

All these are called the PARTS of SPEECH,
Which reading, writing, speaking teach.

—*Helen H. Moore*

Homonyms

Do you hear the difference,
If I say "here" or "hear?"
One's a place that's close to us,
The other you do with your ear.

Use your mind
To think of words
That sound like
They're the same
Like "here" and "hear,"
"Wear" and "ware,"
"No" and "know,"
And "there" and "their."
It makes a funny game!
How many homonyms do you know?
Please play along and don't say "no."

      —Helen H. Moore

Addition

I know that two plus two is four,
And four plus four is eight,
And now that I know how to add,
I want to celebrate!

      —Helen H. Moore

Subtraction

Here is a fact,
I like to subtract!

When I eat lunch,
I subtract when I munch!
Take away one bite,
Take away two,
I am subtracting
Each bite that I chew!

      —Helen H. Moore

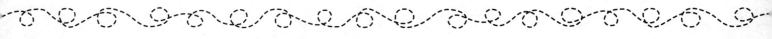

Skip Counting

One, two, three, four, five, six, seven,
Eight, nine, ten's the way we count.

But there is a quicker way
To count the same amount;

Skip counting's what we call it,
Two, four, six, eight, ten.
Skip counting lets us count by twos
Or threes or fours or fives or tens.

Five, ten, fifteen, twenty,
Count a little
Or count plenty.
Twenty-five, thirty,
See how quick
Numbers add up with this trick?

—Helen H. Moore

Cupcake Halves

I had a whole cupcake
And my friend had none,
I cut mine in two equal parts,
And then we each had one—one half!

—Helen H. Moore

Five Flying Kites

Five flying kites, then it started to pour.
Take one down, and now there are four.
Four flying kites, one got stuck in a tree.
Take one down, and now there are three.
Three flying kites, then away one flew.
Take one down, and now there are two.
Two flying kites, one's string came undone.
Take one down, and now there is one.
One flying kite that just wants to play.
I think I'll go fly a kite today!

—Pamela Chanko

Five Little Monkeys

Five little monkeys swinging through the trees.
One fell down and banged his knees.
Mama called the doctor, and he said, "Please!
No more monkeys swinging through the trees!"

Four little monkeys hanging from a vine.
One fell down and began to whine.
Mama called the doctor, and he said, "Fine!
No more monkeys hanging from a vine!"

Three little monkeys climbing up high.
One fell down and began to cry.
Mama called the doctor, and he said, "My!
No more monkeys climbing up high!"

Two little monkeys leaping through the air.
One fell down and bumped a chair.
Mama called the doctor, and he said, "There!
No more monkeys leaping in the air!"

One little monkey jumping high and low.
He fell down and stubbed his toe.
Mama called the doctor, and he said, "So!"
No more monkeys jumping high and low!"

Now there are no little monkeys jumping on the ground.
No little monkeys making any sound.
Mama called the doctor, and he just frowned—
"No more monkeys monkeying around!"

—Pamela Chanko

One Hundred

One hundred pennies in a dollar.
One hundred children give a holler!
One hundred is plenty!
(It's much, much more than twenty!)

—Helen H. Moore

100 Wish

(Note: Fill in the blank with any item.)

If I could have 100
Of anything at all,
I'd love to have 100 _____!
Now, that would be a ball!

—Megan Duhamel

100 Is a Lot!

100 dogs, 100 cats,
100 heads for 100 hats.
100 women, 100 men,
100's more than 5 or 10.
100 buttons, 100 coats,
100 sails for 100 boats.
100 cookies, 100 cakes,
100 kids with bellyaches.
100 shoes, 100 socks,
100 keys for 100 locks.
100 puddles mighty dirty,
100's even more than 30.
100 daughters, 100 sons,
100 franks, 100 buns.
100 trees, 100 plants,
100 picnics, 100 ants.
100 is a lot to count.
100 is a LARGE AMOUNT!
100 kisses, 100 hugs,
100 bats, 100 bugs.
100 bees, 100 birds,
This poem has 100 words!

—Meish Goldish

Money Matters

If you give me a dollar,
And I give you a dime,
Then I'll have a hundred cents of yours,
And you'll have ten of mine!

I'll give you a nickel,
You give me five cents,
Then we'll be even,
And that makes good sense!

—Helen H. Moore

The Number Party

The numbers had a party,
They picked a party place,
They asked the number Zero
To save them each a space.
To which the number Zero
Said, "Sure, I'd be delighted!
'Cause that's the thing that I do best,
I'm glad to be invited!"

Zero ate some party snacks
and party cake and candy.
His big round empty middle
Sure came in very handy!

Zero saved a space for every number at the party;
The Number One came first and said, "I love to party hearty!"
The Number Two came next and said, "I brought a friend with me.
"We go together everywhere—we're just like twins, you see."

Two was barely in the door,
When he was met by Three and Four.
They were joined by Number Five,
Who said, "Come on, let's dance and jive!"

Then there followed Six and Seven,
"This is my idea of heaven!"
Seven said, "Oh, look who's late!"
When she noticed Number Eight.
Number Eight said, "I'm not late!"
and started filling up his plate
With party snacks that tasted fine,
When he noticed Number Nine,
Coming up the walk and then,
Up the path came Number Ten.

"Everybody give a cheer-o,
Let the party start!
Our friend, Zero, is our hero,
He always does his part."

—Helen H. Moore

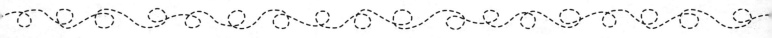

Time Ticks

From the second you wake up,
'Til you close your tired eyes,
Time is ticking,
Time is tocking,
That's why people say it flies!

   —Helen H. Moore

A Minute

Did you know a minute
Has sixty seconds in it?

Stack those minutes like a tower,
Count to sixty, that's an hour.

Twenty-four hours, that's a day,
Time for sleeping, school, and play.

   —Helen H. Moore

Shapes, Colors & Primary Concepts

Shapes All Around

A circle—that's the big bright sun,
Shining down on everyone.
A square—why, that's a window pane,
And every side is just the same.
A triangle's a pizza slice,
Or apple pie is also nice.
A diamond—that's a kite so high,
Flying in the big blue sky.
A rectangle's our classroom door.
Shapes all around—let's find some more!

 —Pamela Chanko

Triangle

It might look like a
Christmas tree,
Or like a pizza slice,

Or maybe like a piece of cheese,
The kind you'd feed to mice.

Can you guess what this shape is?
Just let your mind untangle
These clues and then I bet you'll know
This shape is a triangle.

 —Helen H. Moore

Circle

Round and round,
Round and round,
Look at the circles
That we've found:
A ring, a clock, a cup, a ball,
A planet out in space.
There are circles we can find
All over the place!

 —Helen H. Moore

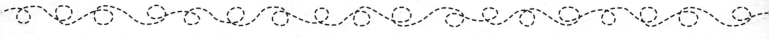

Square

What is a square?
It's a shape that must share
Four corners, four sides
That are all the same size;
That's a square!

   —Helen H. Moore

Color Surprise

Red is a ladybug
There in the grass.
Orange is orange juice
Poured in a glass.

Yellow's the sun,
So high in the sky.
Green is the frog
Who's catching a fly.

Blue is the bluebird
Who's saying "Tweet, tweet."
Purple is violets
That smell very sweet.

Put them all in row
And what do I see?
A beautiful rainbow
For you and for me!

   —Pamela Chanko

Red

Red can be a yo-yo on a string.
Red can be a parrot's wing.

Red can be a fire burning bright.
Red's the color of sunset
when day turns to night.

   —Helen H. Moore

Blue

The sky is blue,
The sea is, too,
Cool and blue.

Blue and cool
Like water in a pool,
Like a bluebell flower,
Like a lonely hour,
Like me without you;
Blue.

   —Helen H. Moore

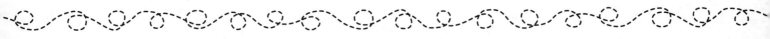

Yellow

Yellow is the color of happy,
Yellow is the color of love,
Yellow is the color of the flowers that grow
And the sun that shines up above.

—Helen H. Moore

What Is Pink?

What is pink? A rose is pink,
By a fountain's brink.
What is red? A poppy's red
In its barley bed.
What is blue? The sky is blue
Where the clouds float through.
What is white? A swan is white,
Sailing in the light.
What is yellow? Pears are yellow,
Rich and ripe and mellow.
What is green? The grass is green,
With small flowers in between.
What is violet? Clouds are violet,
In the summer twilight.
What is orange? Why, an orange,
Just an orange!

—Christina G. Rossetti

Green

Green is for growing things,
Green is for parrots' wings.
Green is the color
Of grass and of trees.
Green is so bright and clean,
I love the color green.
Green is the color for me, if you please!

—Helen H. Moore

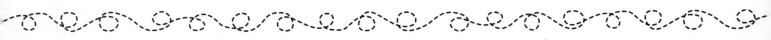

Sizes

Big and little,
Little and big,
Big is a branch, and
Little's a twig!

Little's a kitten,
Big is a cat,
Little's a mouse,
And big is a rat!

—*Helen H. Moore*

High and Low

How low
Does the whale go
When he swims through the ocean
Down below?

How high
Does the eagle fly
When she soars through the clouds
Away up high?

How high or low
Do these animals go?
I don't think I
Can ever know.

But I can wonder
I can look,
And learn about them,
In a book.

—*Helen H. Moore*

Left and Right

It's a bit of a puzzle to me, you see,
The difference between left and right.
It's not like the difference between "up" and "down"
Or even between "black" and "white."

Which side is which—is it left or right?
It's puzzling to me—
It seems to change,
Depending on just where you stand, you see.
If we are standing side by side,
Our left sides are the same.
But when we face each other
Then it's quite a different game!

—*Helen H. Moore*

Opposites

Opposites are different from each other,
Opposites are different as can be.
Opposites are unlike one another,
Opposites are just like A and Z.

Hot and cold, and
Night and day,
Sad and happy,
Work and play—
How many opposites
Can you say?

—*Helen H. Moore*

On the Farm

Living on the Farm

The cows are in the meadow,
The horse is in the barn,
The hens are in the henhouse,
All living on the farm.

Cows give milk that we can drink.
To make us grow up strong.
Hens lay eggs for us to eat,
On the farm where they belong.

—Helen H. Moore

Farm Animals

Cows and pigs and horses,
Chickens on the nest,
Which of these farm animals
Do you like the best?

The sheep are so wooly,
Some white and some black,
The ducks are so funny,
When they go quack, quack!

—Helen H. Moore

Behold the Pig

Behold the pig!
It's very big.
Its color pink
Is nice, I think.
Its tail's a beaut,
So curly cute.
And on the farm,
It oinks with charm.

—Meish Goldish

The Chicken Lays Eggs

Known for its features and wings and legs,
The chicken lays eggs and eggs and eggs!
Known for the comb atop its crown,
The chicken lays eggs of white and brown.
Known for its strut when taking a walk,
The chicken lays eggs! Ba-a-awk! Ba-a-awk!

—Meish Goldish

My Rooster

(Sing to the tune of "My Bonnie")

My rooster, he crows every morning.
He tells me the day is brand-new.
My rooster is up with the sunrise,
To say cock-a-doodle-do!
Wake up, wake up,
Today we have so much to do, to do!
Wake up, wake up,
And say cock-a-doodle, too!

—Pamela Chanko

The Boy in the Barn

A little boy went into the barn,
And lay down on some hay.
An owl came out,
And flew about,
And the little boy ran away.

—Pamela Chanko

Cow

How come a cow
Never says, "Ow,"
Whenever there's milking to do?
It doesn't say, "Boo!"
For it pleases the cow,
So instead, the cow says, "Moo!"

—Meish Goldish

Making Butter

Shake, shake, shake the cream,
Shake it up right now!
Soon we'll have a buttery treat,
Thanks to our friend, the cow!

—Pamela Chanko

Sheepish Sheep

Sheep are rather sheepish,
Sheep are rather shy.
I asked a sheep the reason,
But it wouldn't say why.

—Meish Goldish

Goat

What bearded animal helps on the farm?
The goat!
What friendly creature is loaded with charm?
The goat!
What can produce both milk and wool?
The goat!
What grows long horns like a bull?
The goat!
What creature can mow your lawn?
The goat!
What animal can you always count on?
The goat!

—Meish Goldish

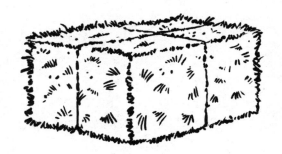

The Farmer's Horse

The farmer's horse is white and gray,
She eats her dinner of grass or hay.

The farmer's horse is strong and smart,
She pulls the farmer along in a cart.

The farmer's horse has big brown eyes.
I bring her an apple—what a surprise!

—Helen H. Moore

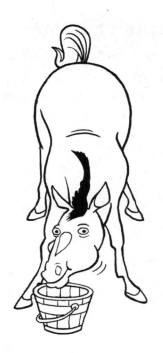

My Horse, of Course!

Who gallops swiftly down the lane,
Slowing to a trot when I pull on the rein?
Who has a tail and a pretty mane?
My horse, of course!

Who nibbles oats and piles of hay?
Who makes the stable his place to say?
Who likes to whinny and say, "Neigh"?
My horse, of course!

—Meish Goldish

A Tiny Mouse

A tiny mouse
Came inside the farmhouse,
Though a tiny crack in the floor.
It stole some cheese
Without saying "Please"
And scampered out the door.

—Meish Goldish

Mammals & More

Mammals, Mammals

Mammals, mammals, everywhere
You don't lay eggs, and
You're covered with hair.
Your blood is warm,
And your lungs breathe air,
Mammals, mammals, everywhere!

—Helen H. Moore

A Trip to the Zoo

Come along, come along,
On a trip to the zoo!
We'll see chattering chimpanzees
And a kangaroo or two!
And a black-and-white zebra
taking a drink
And a golden-maned lion,
And who else do you think?
A spotted giraffe,
Plucking leaves from a tree—
Come along to the zoo
And see them with me!

—Helen H. Moore

Zoo Creatures

All the creatures in the zoo,
Like the snake and kangaroo,
Like the wombat and the bear,
Need our love and all our care.

Next time you're at the zoo,
Watch the creatures watching you.
Do not poke them,
Don't provoke them.
Do not tease them,
Try to please them.
They are creatures,
Just like you,
And they do
What creatures do.
They live and eat and play
In the night and in the day.
Creatures in the zoo,
Please let us learn from you!

—Helen H. Moore

Monkey Meal

In the forest, in the tree,
There's a monkey swinging free.
Hanging by his hands and feet,
Looking for a treat to eat.
Rope bananas growing nearby,
Soon they've caught the monkey's eye.
Monkey grabs one, starts to peel,
Now he's got a monkey meal!

—Meish Goldish

The Hoppy Kangaroo

How do you do, Kangaroo?
You're hoppy, not a grouch.
You hop hop here,
You hop hop there,
With a baby joey in your pouch!

—Meish Goldish

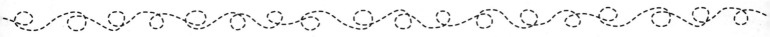

Did You Ever See a Tiger?

(Sing to the tune of "Did You Ever See a Lassie?")

Did you ever see a tiger, a tiger, a tiger,
Did you ever see a tiger, striped this way and that?
Striped this way and that way,
And this way and that way.
No, you've never seen a tiger with stripes quite like that!

   —Pamela Chanko

The Tiger

The tiger is fierce and striped and strong
With claws and teeth so sharp and long!
This cat gets hungry late in the day—
So admire his beauty from far away!

   —Meish Goldish

King of Beasts

The lion is the king of beasts,
It has a mighty roar
And then will rest
For twenty hours more.

The lion roams the grassy plain
With members of its pride.
They sleep and play
Throughout the day
All staying side by side.

The lion is a royal beast,
Its mane is thick and long.
I just can't think
Of another beast
More beautiful or strong.

   —Meish Goldish

Big Brown Bear

Big brown bears are in the woods
Where they like to roam.
All the day they hunt and play
And make a cozy home.

Big brown bears are by the stream,
Lunch is what they wish.
With teeth and paws and sharpened claws,
They plan to catch a fish!

Big brown bears are in their caves,
Where sleeping is their "thing."
They hibernate all winter long
And wake up in the spring!

—Meish Goldish

Polar Bear

Brrr! Brrr! Polar Bear,
Living on the ice,
Your bright, white furry coat
Keeps you warm and nice.

Brrr! Brrr! Polar Bear,
Swimming in the sea,
In freezing waters
You're as happy as can be!

—Meish Goldish

Me and My Polar Bear

My polar bear swims in the ocean.
My polar bear walks on the ice.
I would be cold in the Arctic,
But my polar bear thinks it is nice!

—Pamela Chanko

Bear Family

Bear, bear, bear, bear!
How many kinds of bears are there?
Polar bear and grizzly bear,
Big brown bear with lots of hair!
Spectacled bear, black bear, too,
Sloth bear, sun bear, quite a few!
Bear, bear, bear, bear!
So many bears to compare!

—*Meish Goldish*

Hibernation

In winter when the weather
Just won't behave,
Who's that sleeping
In a big, dark cave?
It's a momma bear,
So furry and warm,
As she sleeps with her babies
Through snow and storm.

—*Helen H. Moore*

Giraffe

Of all the animals walking tall,
The giraffe's the tallest of them all.
Its body stretches very high,
With legs much longer than you or I!
(A giraffe standing on your kitchen floor
Would be three times taller than your door!)
Its legs are long, but if you check,
You'll find an even-longer neck!

—*Meish Goldish*

Spooky Bats

Spooky bats go flying at night,
Flapping about in the pale moonlight.
Spreading their wings, they're a scary sight!
But truth be told, there's no need for fright.

Spooky bats like to sleep in the day.
They hang upside down and doze all day!
Caves and trees are where they stay,
Until it grows dark—then it's up and away!

—*Meish Goldish*

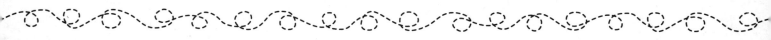

The Elephant

The elephant surely is grand!
It's the largest creature on land!
With jumbo-size ears,
No wonder it hears
For miles from where it stands!

— *Meish Goldish*

The Rhino Song

(Note: Sing to the tune of "Bingo"
and clap each time you encounter a blank.)

Let's sing about an animal,
And rhino is its name-o.
R-H-I-N-O, R-H-I-N-O, R-H-I-N-O,
And rhino is its name-o.

This animal has two horns,
And rhino is its name-o.
_-H-I-N-O, _-H-I-N-O, _-H-I-N-O,
And rhino is its name-o.

This animal eats only plants,
And rhino is its name-o.
_ _-I-N-O, _ _-I-N-O, _ _-I-N-O,
And rhino is its name-o.

Oh, it can grow six feet tall,
And rhino is its name-o.
_ _ _-N-O, _ _ _ -N-O, _ _ _-N-O,
And rhino is its name-o.

And it can weigh 8,000 pounds,
And rhino is its name-o.
_ _ _ _-O, _ _ _ _ _-O, _ _ _ _ _-O,
And rhino is its name-o.

So now you know the rhino song,
And rhino is its name-o.

_ _ _ _ _, _ _ _ _ _ _, _ _ _ _ _,
Yes, rhino is its name-o!

— *Pamela Chanko*

Pets

Pets need food,
Pets need care,
Pets need sunlight,
Pets need air.

Pets need water,
Pets need fun,
Pets need sleep,
Pets need to run.

When we give them
What they need,
Pets give us so much,
Indeed.

Friendship, fun,
Protection, too.
I wish I had a pet,
Don't you?

—Helen H. Moore

Ruff, Ruff

Ruff, ruff! Bow, wow!
My dog's a super pet, and how!
With floppy ears and wagging tail,
He loves to run and fetch the mail!
I toss a bone that's smooth and hard,
He buries it in our backyard!
He's friendly in the neighborhood,
Our neighbors say he's doggone good!
He loves to leap so playfully
And chases squirrels up a tree.
Ruff, ruff! Meow, meow!
Guess who my dog is chasing now?

—Meish Goldish

My Cat

My cat loves to purr
And gently lick her golden fur.
My cat sings "Meow!"
When eating fish and chicken chow!
My cat sharpens her claws
But not on the couch. (She know the laws!)
My cat likes to nap,
And falls asleep right in my lap!
My cat acts purr-fectly
So there is no cat-astrophe!

—Meish Goldish

Question

If grown-ups are strong,
And mice are weak,
Why do mice
Make grown-ups say, "Eek!"

—*Meish Goldish*

The Skunk

Stink! Stank! Stunk!
I think I smell a skunk!
When it's upset, a skunk will spray
To keep its enemies away.
The odor lasts for many days.
Stink! Stank! Stunk!

—*Meish Goldish*

Rabbit

For the rabbit, give three cheers!
One for its long and furry ears!
Two for its short and fluffy tail!
Three for its hop-hop on the trail!
For the rabbit, give three cheers!
Quick, before it disappears!

—*Meish Goldish*

Beware the Porcupine

Beware the porcupine! Beware!
Its body is covered with stiff, sharp hair.
Some good advice with you to share:
Beware the porcupine! Beware!

—*Meish Goldish*

Deer Are Roaming

Deer are roaming in the grass,
In the field I watch them pass.
Deer are grazing on the loose,
Reindeer, red deer, elk, and moose.
Deer with antlers tall and wide,
Royal horns that are worn with pride.
Deer are precious things to see,
Deer are very dear to me.

—*Meish Goldish*

Woodland Animals

Woodland animals live in the woods,
With plenty of trees in their neighborhoods.
The chipmunk, opossum, squirrel, and raccoon
Roam the woods all night and noon.
The bear and fox, the deer and moose,
All woodland creatures on the loose.
Near shores and ponds, and in the water
Are the beavers, muskrats, turtle, and otter.
Woodland animals are up in a tree,
Owls and birds you're sure to see.
Woodland animals like their view
As a woodland creature, wouldn't you?

—Meish Goldish

Whisky, Frisky

Whisky, frisky,
Hippety hop,
Up he goes
To the tree-top!

Whirly, twirly,
Round and round,
Down he scampers
To the ground.

Furry, curly,
What a tail!
Tall as a feather,
Broad as a sail!

Where's his supper?
In the shell,
Snappy, cracky,
Out it fell!

—Author Unknown

A Little Squirrel

I saw a little squirrel,
Sitting in a tree.
He held on tight to a teeny nut
And stared right back at me!

—*Megan Duhamel*

Chipmunk

Hop, skip! Hop, skip! Hop, skip, skip!
Chipmunk's off on a hunting trip.
Hunting for nuts, hunting for seeds.
Hunting for all its winter needs.
Storing the crops in a tunnel below,
Then staying indoors during the winter's snow.
Skip, hop! Skip, hop! Skip, hop, hop!
Smart little chipmunk—store your crop!

—*Meish Goldish*

Baby Animals

Oh, baby, baby, so young and tame,
Oh, baby, baby, so what is your name?
Baby cow is a calf,
Baby deer is a fawn,
Baby goat is a kid eating grass on the lawn.
Baby bear is a cub,
Baby hen is a chick,
Baby swan is a cygnet so graceful and quick.
Baby goose is a gosling,
Baby seal is a pup,
Baby cat is a kitten drinking milk from a cup.
Baby sheep is a lamb,
Baby turkey's a poult,
Baby horse is a foal or filly or colt.
Oh baby, baby, so young and tame,
Oh baby, baby, be proud of your name!

—*Meish Goldish*

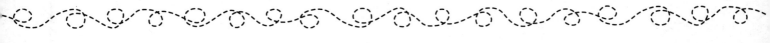

Animal Talk

Ducks quack, bears growl,
Geese honk, wolves howl.
Hens cluck, horses neigh,
Bees buzz, donkeys bray.

Cats meow, dogs bark,
Birds chirp in the park.
Turkeys gobble, cows moo,
Tigers roar in the zoo.

Snakes hiss, pigs squeal,
Hyenas laugh a great deal.
Owls hoot, mice squeak,
Animals love to speak!

—*Meish Goldish*

Home, Sweet Animal Home

Birds like to rest
In a twiggy nest.
A big brown bear
Prefers a lair.
Bats love to rave
About their cave!
Monkeys swing free
High in a tree!
The tiny frog
Lives on a log.
Chipmunks are found
In a hole on the ground.
Home in a thicket?
A lion would pick it!
The hermit crab lives well
Inside an empty shell.
A hive would please
A family of bees.
Is your home a home
For dogs or cats?
Animals have many habitats!

—*Meish Goldish*

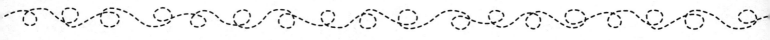

Backyard Animals

Rabbits and fish,
Ferrets and llamas,
Potbellied pigs,
And their potbellied mamas,

There's grass for the rabbits,
A pond for the fish,
Some mud for the pigs,
For the ferret, a dish.

The llama is so gentle,
It isn't very hard.
To see why I love
My animal backyard.

—Helen H. Moore

Animals From A to Z

A is Ape, B is Bee,
C is Clownfish in the sea!

D is Deer, E is Eel,
F's a Fox who wants a meal.

G is Goose, H is Hog,
I's an Inchworm on a log.

Jay is J, Koala's K,
L's a Lion far away.

M is Mule, N is Newt,
O's an Ostrich, tall and cute.

P is Pig, Q is Quail,
R's a Rat with a curly tail.

Snake is S, Turkey's T,
U's the Umbrella bird flying free.

V is Viper, Worm is W,
Bird "X" are you hatching?
(Does that joke trouble you?)

Yak is Y, Zebra's Z
Alphabet animals for you and me!

—Meish Goldish

Rainforest Friends

Rainforest animals,
Rainforest trees,
Toucans and jaguars,
Butterflies and bees,
Gorillas,
Orangutans,
Cassowarries,
Lemurs,
And tigers, and
Rainforest trees.

—Helen H. Moore

In the Rainforest

Where can you find a toucan?
In the rainforest, you can!
High on a limb is where it
Can be seen with the monkey and parrot.
Squirrels leap from tree to tree,
While bats go flying free.
There's a bee, mosquito, and moth,
Look up! See the hanging sloth!
Down on the forest floor
Are big and small creatures galore:
The tapir, snake, and frog,
Plus termites and ants on a log.
Every day, hour by hour,
Butterflies float on a flower.
Colorful lizards also play
In the tall green plants each day.
Ocelots, jaguars, leopards—yes!
The rainforest is a popular address!

—Meish Goldish

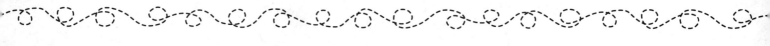

Remarkable Reptiles & Awesome Amphibians

What Is a Reptile?

Reptiles are crocodiles,
Turtles and snakes.
To be called a reptile
Here's what it takes:
Be a cold-blooded creature,
Have dry, scaly skin;
Breathe with your lungs
Breathe out and breathe in.

Reptiles are alligators,
Tortoises, and lizards,
Hiding in the desert
From hot, sandy blizzards.
Some say that dinosaurs
Were reptiles long ago.
What is a reptile?
Well, now you know!

—Meish Goldish

Reptile Party

We're having a reptile party,
And you're invited, too.
The reptiles party hearty
When the people leave the zoo.

The crocodile
Begins to smile,
The snake begins to slither,
The lizard drums the turtles' backs,
And the gecko plays the zither!

—Helen H. Moore

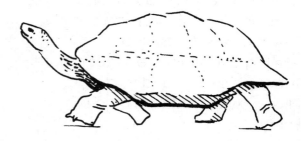

If You Smile at a Crocodile

The crocodile
Has a toothy smile,
His teeth are sharp and long.
And in the swamp
When he takes a chomp
His bite is quick and strong!

So if you smile
At a crocodile,
There's just one thing to say:
If he smiles too,
Be sure that you
Are VERY far away!

  —Meish Goldish

Crocodile

If you should meet a crocodile
Don't take a stick and poke him.
Ignore the welcome in his smile,
Be careful not to poke him.

For as he sleeps upon the Nile
He gets thinner and thinner.
And whenever you meet a crocodile,
He's ready for his dinner.

  —Author Unknown

So Many Snakes

For heaven's sake, so many snakes!
Garter snakes, cobras,
Milk snakes, rat snakes,
Copperheads, pythons,
Thin snakes, fat snakes,
King snakes, bull snakes,
Water snakes, rat snakes
Vipers and rattlesnakes!
For heaven's sakes, so many snakes!

  —Meish Goldish

Rattlesnake

Rattle, rattle, rattlesnake,
Rattle on the ground.
Beware if there's a rattlesnake
Rattling around!

  —Meish Goldish

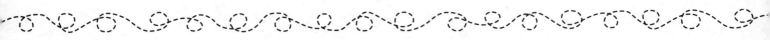

Amphibian

Amphibian, you're not like me.
You were born in a pond or the salty sea.
Now that you're grown, you live on land,
In the grassy grass,
Or the sandy sand.
You might be a frog, or a toad, or a newt,
Or a chameleon, green and cute.
Or a salamander you might be,
But amphibian, you're not like me.

—Helen H. Moore

Frog Song

On a lily-pad throne,
You float like a king.
Then when it gets dusky,
You start to sing:
Ribbity ribbit croakity croak,
Ribbity ribbit croakity croak—

I love every sandpaper note!

—Liza Charlesworth

Lizard

Lizard in the desert,
Lizard on the ground,
Lizard climbing rocks
And scampering around.

Chameleon's a lizard,
So is the iguana.
If you could be a lizard,
Do you think you'd wanna?

—Meish Goldish

Birds, Birds, Birds

So Many Birds

Birds in the sky, in the lake, in the tree,
So many birds for you to see!
Mockingbird, blue jay, robin, sparrow,
Cardinal, oriole, swift as an arrow!
Bobolink, chickadee, bullfinch, crow,
Warbler, raven, watch them go!
Meadowlark, blackbird, nightingale, thrush,
Birds in a bush, and birds in the brush.
Woodpecker, hummingbird, osprey, owl,
Chicken and turkey (known as fowl).
Duck in the water, dove in the sky,
Ostrich and penguin, which don't even fly!
Swan and pelican, puffin and goose,
Buzzard and eagle on the loose.
Stork and heron with long thin legs,
Hawk and falcon, guarding their eggs.
Albatross, vulture, peacock, pheasant,
Birds that are wild, birds that are pleasant.
Birds in the sky, in the lake, in the tree,
So many birds for you to see!

—Meish Goldish

Migration

What calendar,
What compass,
Do birds own

That lets them know

It's time
To go?

—Helen H. Moore

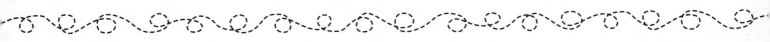

There Was a Little Robin

There was a little robin
Sat singing in a tree;
From early morn till dark he sang—
"The world was made for me!"

—*Wilhelmina Seegmuller*

Sing, Little Bird

Sing, little bird, when the skies are blue,
Sing, for the world has need of you,
Sing when the skies are overcast,
Sing when the rain is falling fast.

Sing, happy heart, when the sun is warm,
Sing in the winter's coldest storm,
Sing, little songs, O heart so true,
Sing, for the world has need of you.

—*Author Unknown*

Penguin

Penguin cold and
Penguin cute,
Waddling in your
Penguin suit!

Laying eggs and
Swimming fast,
Penguins, penguins,
Have a blast!

—*Helen H. Moore*

Best-Dressed Bird

The penguin's a bird that cannot fly
But can swim like a torpedo.
And on the ice
It looks so nice
Dressed in its own tuxedo!

—*Meish Goldish*

Parrots

Red and blue and orange and green,
Parrots have feathers like you've never seen!
The white-feathered cockatoo's a friendly fellow,
Wearing a beautiful crown of yellow!
The scarlet macaw is a bird to hail
With an orange-red, long, and very straight tail!
The rainbow lorikeet flies quite high
And looks like a rainbow in the sky!

—*Meish Goldish*

The Eagle

The eagle is a noble bird
With features bald and bold.
It soars with pride
On wings so wide,
With beak and claws of gold.

The eagle is our nation's bird,
Flying proud and free.
If I could fly
Up in the sky,
An eagle's what I'd be!

—*Meish Goldish*

Gobble, Gobble, Gobble!

The turkey likes to walk about,
Wobble, wobble, wobble.
He also likes to talk a lot—
Gobble, gobble, gobble!

—*Megan Duhamel*

Runaway Ducks

Four little ducks went out one day,
Over the hill and far away.
Mother duck said,
"Quack, quack, quack, quack!"
And the four little ducks
Came quacking back!

  —*Author Unknown*

The Owl Cheer

H is for hearing the sound of night.
O is for owl eyes, shining so bright!
O is for owlets, all safe in their nests.
T is for talons—beware, owl guests!

Put them together and what do they spell?
It's the song of the owl we know so well!
So sing to the owls, call out your salute—
In the forest at night, you might hear a... HOOT!

  —*Pamela Chanko*

Owl Eyes

Owl eyes,
Owl eyes,
What do you see,
As you fly through the night,
So silent and free?
You see in the darkness,
You sleep in the day,
At night you go hunting,
In feathers brown and grey.

  —*Helen H. Moore*

Graceful Swan

Graceful in the water,
Graceful in the sky,
Moving, oh, so gracefully,
The swan is gliding by.

  —*Meish Goldish*

Creepy Crawlies

Insects

Insects, insects everywhere,
In the earth and in the air,

Beetles brown and green and black
With tiny legs and shiny back,

Ants and aphids, termites, too
Doing what they're made to do,

Bees that bumble, flies that buzz,
Each one knows just what she does,

Insects, insects everywhere,
On earth and sky and sea,
each one has a place to be
In our earth's ecology.

—Helen H. Moore

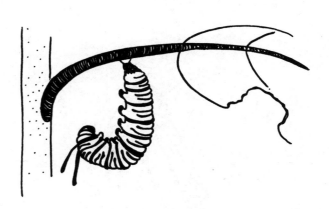

Caterpillar

Brown and furry
Caterpillar in a hurry,
Take your walk
To the shady leaf, or stalk,
Or what not,
Which may be the chosen spot.
No toad spy you,
Hovering bird of prey pass by you;
Spin and die,
To live again a butterfly.

—Christina G. Rossetti

Ugh, a Bug!

Ugh, a bug under my rug!
Now it's on the floor.
Now it's crawling across the room,
Now it's out the door!

—Meish Goldish

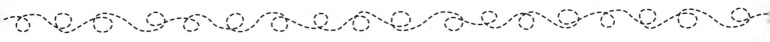

Growing Butterfly

What is this?
It's a chrysalis,
Hanging from a flower.
Inside,
A future butterfly
Is growing by the hour!

—Helen H. Moore

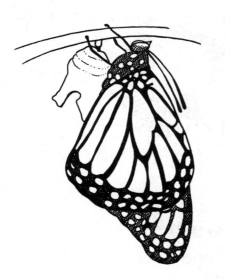

Butterfly Garden

Flutter, flutter! What do you see?
Five bright butterflies flying free!
It would be nice if they would stay—
But, flutter, flutter, one sails away.
Then four butterflies are left to play.

—Megan Duhamel

(Note: Create math problems
by changing the numbers in
lines 2, 4, and 5.)

Butterflies Go Fluttering

Butterflies go fluttering by
On colored wings that catch the eye.
On wings of orange, and silvery blue,
On wings of golden yellow, too.
Butterflies float in the air,
Making their homes most anywhere:
The rainforest, field, and prairie land,
On mountaintops, and desert sand.
If winter brings the cold and snow,
To warmer climates, off they go!
Returning home the following spring,
Beautiful butterflies on the wing!

—Meish Goldish

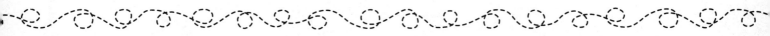

Hop! Hop! Hop!

Hop! Hop! Hop!
My, what strength!
A grasshopper hops
Twenty times its length!
Farmer says, "Grasshopper,
Stay off my crop!"
There goes the grasshopper,
Hop! Hop! Hop!

—*Meish Goldish*

In the Beehive

Here is the beehive,
But where are the bees?
Hidden inside, where nobody sees.
Watch as they come out of their hive,
One, two, three bees,
Four bees, five!

—*Author Unknown*

Buzzy Bee

BUZZ! Goes the bee,
Hour after hour,
BUZZ! Goes the bee
From flower to flower.

Sucking out the nectar,
Flying it home.
Storing up the nectar
In the honeycomb!

BUZZ! Goes the bee,
Making honey so sweet.
Bee makes the honey
That I like to eat!

—*Meish Goldish*

Ants Are Marching

The ants are marching in a row.
Ants! Ants! Ants! Ants!
In their colony, off they go.
Ants! Ants! Ants! Ants!
Army ants go out for prey.
Ants! Ants! Ants! Ants!
Harvester ants store seeds all day.
Ants! Ants! Ants! Ants!
Honey ants eat honeydew.
Ants! Ants! Ants! Ants!
Carpenter ants find wood to chew.
Ants! Ants! Ants! Ants!
Amazon ants and bulldog ants,
Ants in picnics, ants in plants.
Ants! Ants! Ants! Ants!

—Meish Goldish

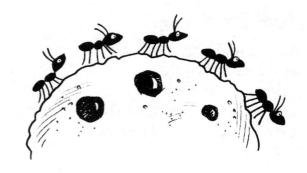

Ladybug

Round and red,
Round and red,
Ladybug in my flower bed.
Red and round,
Red and round,
Ladybug, ladybug, on the ground.

—Helen H. Moore

Pesky Mosquito

Pesky mosquito,
Please fly away!
Your itchy-scratchy bites
Are ruining my day!

—Meish Goldish

June Bug

June bug, June bug,
Please reply:
What do they call you
In July?

—*Meish Goldish*

Glowing Fireflies

Glowing, glowing in the night,
Fireflies shine a yellow light.
I wish I may, I wish I might
See some fireflies tonight!

—*Meish Goldish*

Wiggle, Wiggle

Wiggle, wiggle, squiggle, squiggle,
Wiggly, squiggy worm.
With no backbone, with no legs
How you twist and squirm!

—*Meish Goldish*

Spider Friend

Spiders, spiders
On silky threads—
You decorate dull corners
With lovely, lacy webs!

—*Liza Charlesworth*

In the Deep Blue Sea

Ocean Animals

Under the waves,
Down deep in the sea,
Live animals different
From you and from me.

Manatees, walruses,
Dolphins and seals,
Starfishes, sea urchins,
Lobsters and eels!

They live in the water,
They don't live on land,
Some swim and some float
And some crawl on the sand.

—Helen H. Moore

What Do You See in the Sea?

What do you see in the sea?
Animals moving free!
Snails and whales
Using their tails.
Seals and eels
Looking for meals.
Catfish, flatfish
Chasing fat fish.
What do you see in the sea?
Animals moving free!

—Meish Goldish

Wonderful Water World

Darting and dashing
In water so deep,
Do you close your eyes
When you go to sleep?
Or do they stay open,
The better to see,
That wonderful water world
Under the sea?

—Helen H. Moore

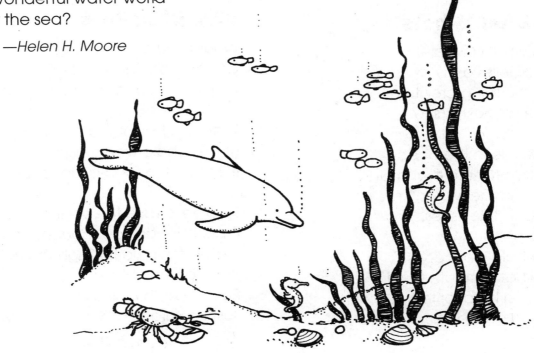

Seal, Seal

Seal, seal, in the sea,
Flapping flippers, swimming free.
Seal, seal, on the ice,
The whiskers on your lip are nice.
Seal, seal, in the zoo,
My seal of approval goes to you!

—Meish Goldish

Something Fishy

Fishes in the sea
Are in a school, like me.
They swim and go,
To and fro,
Swimming fast,
Swimming slow.
Fishes in the sea,
Swimming happy,
Swimming free.

—Helen H. Moore

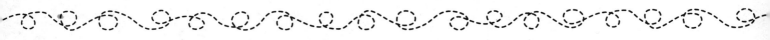

Clam

On the ocean floor,
The clam's in its shell,
And there it's protected
Very well!

—Meish Goldish

Big Blue Whale

Wow, what a whale!
I can't believe my eyes!
Of all the living creatures,
It's the biggest in size.

Blue whale in the ocean
Swims anywhere it wishes.
Moving in the water,
Look out, little fishes!

Blue whale is hungry,
And what a mouth to fill!
Dining on its favorite treat:
Seafood called krill.

Blue whale in the ocean,
Blue whale in the sea,
Of all living creatures,
It's the biggest there can be!

—Meish Goldish

Whale Sailing

Would you go for a sail
On the back of a whale?
Would you sail through the ocean so blue?

There's a lot you could see
(If the whale would agree),
It's more fun than a trip to the zoo!

So please take the chance,
If the chance you should get,
To ride a whale through the ocean.
You'll get mighty wet,
But it's worth it, you bet.
Just be sure to rub on suntan lotion!

—Helen H. Moore

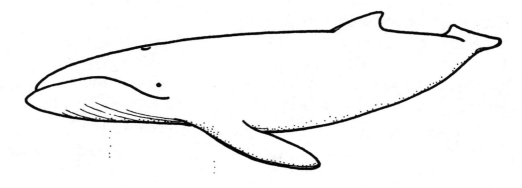

Dolphin

Dolphin wild and
Dolphin free,
Dolphin swimming
In the sea,
You're a mammal,
Just like me!

—Helen H. Moore

Hark, a Shark!

Hark, a shark,
so fast and fierce,
is swimming in the sea!
Hark, a shark,
so fast and fierce,
please stay away from me!

—Megan Duhamel

Octopus

The arms on an octopus number eight:
One, two, three, four, five, six, seven, eight!
All curled up, then pointing straight,
One, two, three, four, five, six, seven, eight!
In the ocean, octopuses wait,
One, two, three, four, five, six, seven, eight!
For clams and crabs to put on their plate!
One, two, three, four, five, six, seven, eight!

—Meish Goldish

At the Sea-side

When I was down beside the sea
A wooden spade they gave to me
To dig the sandy shore.
My holes were empty like a cup,
In every hole the sea came up,
Till it could come no more.

—*Robert Louis Stevenson*

Sand

Sand in my swimsuit,
Sand in my hair,
When I go to the beach,
Sand gets everywhere!

I wonder, I wonder,
Oh, how can there be
Sand left at the beach
When there's so much on me?

—*Helen H. Moore*

Ocean Motion

There's a motion
In the ocean,
Waves that tower
Overhead.

Ocean motion,
Rolling over
Rocks and sand
On the sea bed.

—*Helen H. Moore*

Tides

Water is wet,
Sand is dry,
When tides are low
And tides are high.

We see more water
When tides are high,
When tides are low,
It's sand we spy!

—*Helen H. Moore*

Earth & Beyond

Our Beautiful World

Sunlight and starlight,
Moonlight and soft breeze,
Cloudy skies, sunny skies,
Rivers and trees,
Our beautiful world
Has so many of these!
Aren't you happy?
Isn't it fun?
To live in a beautiful world
Like this one?

—Helen H. Moore

Blue Marble Earth

Earth is like a marble
Blue, white, and green,
The prettiest marble
I've ever seen.

—Helen H. Moore

The Sun

The sun is just
A great big star,
So close that we can see.
It shines on rocks,
And grass, and trees,
It shines on you and me!

—Helen H. Moore

Goodnight Sun

The sun slides down
The west of the sky,
From the perch it held
At noon, so high.
And at sunset it pauses,
To tell us goodnight,
And it turns off daytime
then turns out the light.

—Helen H. Moore

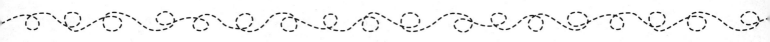

Sometimes the Moon

Sometimes the moon is round as a ball.
It shines down brightly on us all!

Sometimes the moon is just half there.
Its other half must have gone somewhere!

Sometimes the moon is thin as a string.
It hardly lights up anything!

Sometimes the moon isn't there to see!
It doesn't shine on you or me!

Whatever its size or shape or shine,
The moon's a special friend of mine!

—Helen H. Moore

Moon Changes

The moon looks different
Every night
As it waxes and wanes
And shines so bright.

Full moon, half moon,
Crescent moon, then
Moon phases start
All over again!

—Helen H. Moore

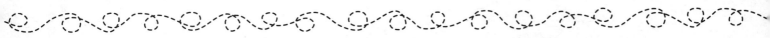

Sun and Moon Sisters

It's morning time!
The sun says, "Hi!"
As she opens the day,
Way up in the sky.

And after the daytime
Comes the night,
When the moon shines down
Her silvery light.

The sun and moon are sisters,
Each one is oh, so bright.
Sun sister says, "Good morning,"
Moon sister says, "Sleep tight!"

—Helen H. Moore

Our Solar System

Mercury is near the sun,
Venus shines so bright,
Earth's the planet we call home,
Mars has a reddish light.

Jupiter's the biggest of the planets
In our system;
Name the rest
And show you've got
Some planetary wisdom:
You know Neptune, Saturn and Uranus,
And please don't avoid
Tiny Pluto—
It's so small,
It's called a planetoid!

—Helen H. Moore

Our Space Neighbors

One sun,
Seven planets,
A moon
And Earth,
Living here in space,

One sun,
Seven planets,
And Earth,
We keep a dizzy pace!

       —Helen H. Moore

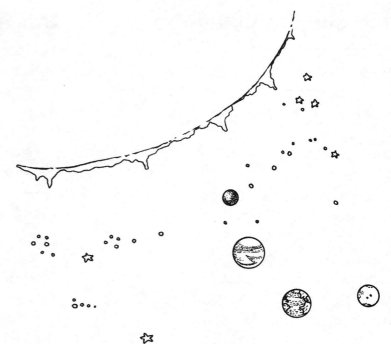

Stars

When the wind blows the clouds
Across the blue sky, and the sun shines with all of its might,
We can't see the stars, though we know that they're there,
We can only see starshine at night.

The stars are so far from us here on the Earth,
That they seem oh, so tiny and bright,
As they shimmer and shine, like a diamond design
In the black velvet cloak of the night.

       —Helen H. Moore

Science & Nature

Apple Tree Cycle

In summer tiny buds appear,
They grow all summer long.
In fall they grow a fuzzy coat,
To keep them warm and strong.
In winter apple tree buds sleep,
Their blossom-secret growing.
In springtime buds turn into leaves,
Soon pretty flowers are showing.
Insects come to pollinate
Each pretty apple blossom,
Then apples grow,
With seeds inside,
I think that's really awesome!

—Helen H. Moore

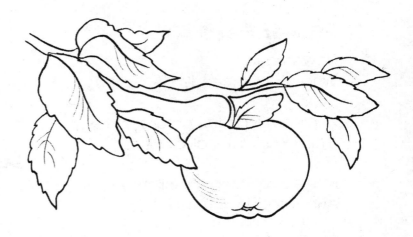

Apple Riddle

What do I want to eat?
Something crisp and sweet?
Something round and red?
Or sometimes green instead?
Yes!
An apple is the treat
That I would like to eat!

—Helen H. Moore

Apples

Apples, apples, what a treat,
Sweet and tart and good to eat.
Apples green and apples red,
Hang from branches overhead,
And when they ripen
Down they drop,
So we can taste our apple crop.

—Helen H. Moore

Flower Seed

Flower seed,
What do you need?

I'll plant you in the ground,
Then pour water all around,

Make sure you get sunlight,
And what do you know?

My lovely little garden
Will grow and grow and grow!

—Helen H. Moore

In the Garden

Butterflies and bumblebees,
Ladybugs and flowers,
For a garden full of these
We must have rain showers.

Rain showers bring water.
And when the sky is clear,
Sunshine brings the
Things we love to see and smell
and hear:
Bumblebees that buzz, buzz, buzz,
The flowers that smell so sweet,
The butterflies and ladybugs that
Creep on teeny feet.

—Helen H. Moore

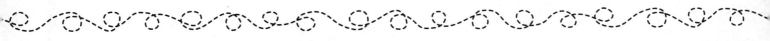

Pumpkin Magic

Plant some pumpkin seeds,
Take care of all their needs.
Give them water and sun,
Then watch all the fun.
See the pumpkin sprout?
Soon the flower will come out
Of the pumpkin vine.
Keep it watered just fine,
Soon you'll see a pumpkin ball,
So green and so small
(It almost doesn't look like a pumpkin at all).
But then what do you know,
That ball begins to grow!
A change starts taking place;
Green turns to orange at a pumpkin's pace!
And pretty soon we'll have a patch
Of pumpkins all over the place!

—Helen H. Moore

Extinct Animals

Extinct animals no longer survive.
Not one of their kind is alive.
Once, for example, dinosaurs were here,
Until each one seems to disappear.
The dodo bird, the mammoth, too,

And the passenger pigeon are just a few
Of extinct animals who live no more.
They've taught us a lesson we can't ignore:
Let's care for the animals living today,
Don't take their homes or their shelters away!
Show them respect, and help them last
So extinct animals are a thing of the past!

—Meish Goldish

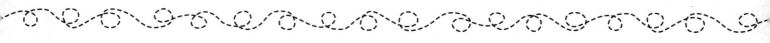

When Dinosaurs Walked the Earth

(Sing to the tune of "When Johnny Comes Marching Home")

The dinosaurs came out to play,
Hurrah, hurrah!
The carnivores ate meat all day,
Hurrah, hurrah!
The herbivores ate up the plants,
Then all the dinos did a dance.
It was long ago, when dinosaurs walked the Earth.

Some dinosaurs had pointy backs,
Hurrah, hurrah!
Some dinosaurs made giant tracks,
Hurrah, hurrah!
Some dino's necks reached so high,
You'd think that they could touch the sky.
It was long ago, when dinosaurs walked the Earth.

The dinosaurs were big and strong,
Hurrah, hurrah!
But then the dinos said, "So long!"
Hurrah, hurrah!
What happened is a mystery.
A dinosaur you'll never see,
'Cause they're all gone now.
No dinosaurs left on Earth.

—Pamela Chanko

Dinosaurus No More-Us

Tyrannosaurus, did you roar?
Pterodactyl, did you soar?
Ankylosaurus, could you think?
Maiasaura, were you pink?

There's so much we don't know for sure,
Like were you pink?
How loud was your roar?
We'll never really know for sure,
Because you're not here anymore!

—Helen H. Moore

Food & Fun

Fruits and Veggies

Please pass the fruits and veggies,
I love them 'cause I know,
That fruits and veggies are the foods
I need to help me grow.

—*Helen H. Moore*

The Ketchup Bottle

When you tip
the ketchup bottle,
first
comes
out
a
little,
then a whole lottle!

—*Helen H. Moore*

Popcorn

Pop, pop, popcorn,
Popping in the pot!
Pop, pop, popcorn,
eat it while it's hot.

Pop, pop, popcorn,
Butter on the top!
When I eat popcorn,
I can't stop!

—*Helen H. Moore*

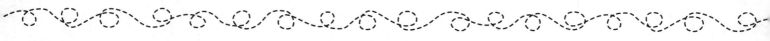

Pizza Pizzazz

Have you ever seen a more delicious sight
Than a pizza dressed up to go out at night?
Thick tomato sauce and mozzarella cheese,
mushrooms and sausage, more peppers, please!
Onions, olives, choice pepperoni!
Anything goes, just hold the anchovies!
Top it all off with a sprinkle of spice.
It's looking so good—Hey, who took a slice?

    —Liza Charlesworth

Ice Cream

Ice cream, ice cream,
Cold and sweet,
On a hot summer day,
It can't be beat,
In a cone or a cup
It's my favorite treat.
In a sundae, or sandwich,
I want one-in-each-handwich,
With sprinkles on top,
Or whipped cream and a cherry,
Vanilla or chocolate, or even
strawberry,
Ice cream makes my
Mouth so merry!

    —Helen H. Moore

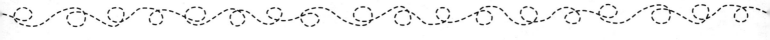

The Gingerbread Man Song

(Sing to the tune of "The Wheels on the Bus," substituting the new line in each verse)

Chorus:
Run, run, run, as fast as you can,
Fast as you can, fast as you can!
Run, run, run, as fast as you can,
You can't catch the Gingerbread Man!

Verse 1:
He ran from the man, he ran and ran,
Ran and ran, ran and ran!
He ran from the man, he ran and ran!
You can't catch the Gingerbread Man!

(Chorus)

Verse 2:
He ran from the woman…
(Chorus)

Verse 3:
He ran from the cow…
(Chorus)

Verse 4:
He ran from the pig…
(Chorus)

Verse 5:
He ran from the horse…

(Chorus)

Verse 6:
He ran from them all, he ran and ran,
Ran and ran, ran and ran!
Then came a fox, who had a plan—
GULP!
No more Gingerbread Man!

      —Pamela Chanko

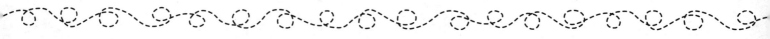

Myself and the Elf

I was walking in the woods one day,
Walking by myself.
I heard a noise along the way,
And there I saw an elf!

His cape was brown,
His hair was gold,
His shoes and socks were yellow.
I wish I'd see that elf again,
He was a funny fellow.

    —Helen H. Moore

Cat and Dog

If only the cat had sat,
And stayed there on her mat,
Then that would have been that.

But oh, no, not my cat,
She got right up and sat
On the dog's new mat,
And then, there was a spat!
And that was really that!

    —Helen H. Moore

Soon

I asked my dad
If I could fly
Away up to
The moon.

My dad said,
Yes, my little one,
You'll go there
Very soon.

I asked my dad
How I could go
Away up to the moon.
My dad said that
He'd take me there,
In his hot-air balloon!

    —Helen H. Moore

Mystery Sounds

Did you hear that?
I heard it, too!
I wonder what it is?
Do you?

Did it sound like roaring thunder?
Or like something from down under?
Did it purr just like a cat,
As it sits upon its mat?
Did it croak just like a frog,
Sitting there upon a log?
Did it hiss just like a snake,
Swimming in a green, green lake?
Which way did that strange sound go?
Did it sound high?
Did it sound low?
Will we ever, ever know?
It's gone now, so I don't think so!
Oh-oh.

—Helen H. Moore

The Red Ball

The red ball
slipped from
The baby's hands,
bounced,
    bounced,
       bounced,
down the cement stairs,
zoomed past
a fire hydrant,
raced through
a championship game
of hopscotch,
crossed the street,
rolled under
a blue car,
then zigzagged between
two dozen pairs
of feet,
until one sneaker
kicked it up
into the air
with such force
it landed
with a PLUNK!
in the tidy nest of a jay,
who, by the way,
is still waiting
for the curious thing
to hatch.

—Liza Charlesworth

Is That an Owl?

Is that an owl,
Hiding under a towel?
I don't think it is
'Cause I heard it growl!

—Helen H. Moore

139

Mother Goose & Classic Rhymes

Baa, Baa, Black Sheep

Baa, baa, black sheep,
  Have you any wool?
Yes sir, yes sir,
  Three bags full.
One for my master,
  One for my dame,
And one for the little boy
  That lives in our lane.

Fiddling Cat

A cat came fiddling out of a barn,
With a pair of bagpipes under her arm.
She could sing nothing but fiddle dum dee,
The mouse has married the bumblebee.

Cobbler, Cobbler

Cobbler, cobbler, mend my shoe,
Give it a stitch and that will do.
Here's a nail, and there's a prod,
And now my foot is well shod.

Diddle, Diddle, Dumpling

Diddle, diddle, dumpling, my son John
Went to bed with his stockings on;
One shoe off, and one shoe on,
Diddle, diddle, dumpling, my son John.

Bumpety, Bumpety, Bump

A farmer went riding
Upon his gray mare;
Bumpety, bumpety, bump!
With his daughter behind him,
So rosy and fair;
Lumpety, lumpety, lump!
A raven cried, "Croak!"
And they all tumbled down;
Bumpety, bumpety, bump!
The mare broke her knees,
And the farmer his crown;
Lumpety, lumpety, lump!
The mischievous raven
Flew laughing away;
Bumpety, bumpety, bump!
And vowed he would serve them
The same the next day;
Lumpety, lumpety, lump!

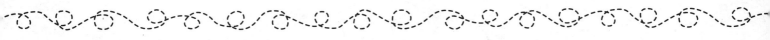

Boys and Girls

Girls and boys, come out to play,
The moon is shining as bright as day.
Leave your supper, and leave your sleep,
And come with your playfellows into the street.
Come with a whoop, come with a call,
Come with a good will or not at all.
Up the ladder and down the wall,
A halfpenny roll will serve us all.
You find milk, and I'll find flour,
And we'll have pudding in half an hour.

Hey, Diddle, Diddle

Hey, diddle, diddle,
The cat and the fiddle,
The cow jumped over the moon;
The little dog laughed
To see such sport,
And the dish ran away with the spoon.

Hickory, Dickory, Dock

Hickory, dickory, dock,
The mouse ran up the clock,
The clock struck one,
The mouse ran down,
Hickory, dickory, dock.

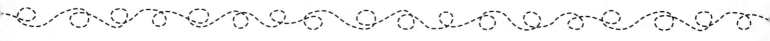

My Black Hen

Higgledy, piggledy, my black hen,
She lays eggs for gentlemen;
Sometimes nine, sometimes ten,
Higgledy, piggledy, my black hen.

Humpty-Dumpty

Humpty-Dumpty sat on a wall,
Humpty-Dumpty had a great fall;
All the king's horses and all the king's men
Could not put Humpty together again.

Rock-a-Bye, Baby

Rock-a-bye, baby,
   In the tree top,
When the wind blows,
   The cradle will rock.
When the bough breaks,
   The cradle will fall,
And down will come baby,
   Cradle and all.

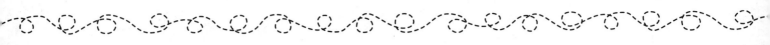

The Little Nut Tree

I had a little nut tree, nothing would it bear
But a silver nutmeg and a golden pear.
The king of Spain's daughter came to visit me,
And all for the sake of my little nut tree.
I skipped over water, I danced over sea,
And all the birds in the air couldn't catch me.

Jack and Jill

Jack and Jill went up the hill
To fetch a pail of water.
Jack fell down, and broke his crown,
And Jill came tumbling after.
Up Jack got
And home did trot
As fast as he could caper,
Went to bed
To mend his head
With vinegar and brown paper.

Jack Be Nimble

Jack be nimble,
Jack be quick,
Jack jump over
The candlestick.

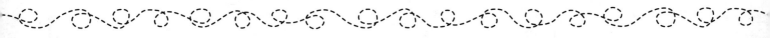

Little Betty Blue

Little Betty Blue
Lost her holiday shoe.
What can little Betty do?
Give her another
To match the other,
And then she may walk in two.

Little Bo-Peep

Little Bo-peep has lost her sheep,
And can't tell where to find them;
Leave them alone, and they'll come home,
And bring their tails behind them.
Little Bo-peep fell fast asleep,
And dreamt she heard them bleating;
But when she awoke, she found it a joke,
For they were still a-fleeting.
Then up she took her little crook,
Determined for to find them;
She found them indeed, but it made her heart bleed,
For they'd left all their tails behind them.

Little Boy Blue

Little Boy Blue, come blow your horn.
The sheep's in the meadow, the cow's in the corn.
Where is the boy that looks after the sheep?
"He's under the haycock, fast asleep."
Will you wake him? "No, not I;
For if I do, he'll be sure to cry."

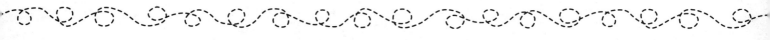

Little Jack Horner

Little Jack Horner
Sat in a corner,
Eating his Christmas pie.
He put in his thumb,
And he pulled out a plum,
And said, "What a good boy am I!"

Little Miss Muffet

Little Miss Muffet
Sat on a tuffet,
Eating of curds and whey.
There came a spider,
And sat down beside her,
And frightened Miss Muffet away.

Mistress Mary, Quite Contrary

Mistress Mary, quite contrary,
How does your garden grow?
With cockle-shells, and silver bells,
And pretty maids all in a row.

The North Wind

The north wind doth blow,
And we shall have snow,
And what will the robin do then?
Poor thing!
He will sit in a barn,
And to keep himself warm,
Will hide his head under his wing.
Poor thing!

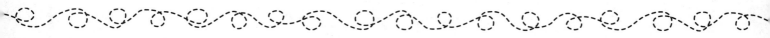

Old King Cole

Old King Cole
Was a merry old soul,
And a merry old soul was he;
He called for his pipe,
And he called for his bowl,
And he called for his fiddlers three.
Each fiddler, he had a fiddle,
And a very fine fiddle had he;
Oh, there's none so rare,
As can compare
With King Cole and his fiddlers three!

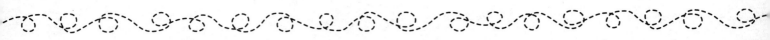

Old Mother Hubbard

Old Mother Hubbard
Went to the cupboard
To get her poor dog a bone;
But when she came there
The cupboard was bare,
And so the poor dog had none.

She went to the baker's
To buy him some bread;
But when she came back
The poor dog was dead.

She went to the joiner's
To buy him a coffin;
But when she came back
The poor dog was laughing.

She took a clean dish,
To get him some tripe;
But when she came back
He was smoking his pipe.

She went to the hatter's
To buy him a hat;
But when she came back
He was feeding the cat.

She went to the barber's
To buy him a wig;
But when she came back
He was dancing a jig.

She went to the fruiterer's
To buy him some fruit;
But when she came back
He was playing the flute.

She went to the tailor's
To buy him a coat;
But when she came back
He was riding a goat.

She went to the cobbler's
To buy him some shoes;
But when she came back
He was reading the news.

She went to the seamstress
To buy him some linen;
But when she came back
The dog was spinning.

She went to the hosier's
To buy him some hose;
But when she came back
He was dressed in his clothes.

The dame made a curtsey,
The dog made a bow;
The dame said, "Your servant,"
The dog said, "Bow-wow."

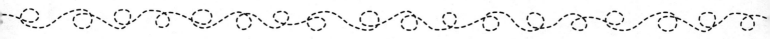

Little Bird

Once I saw a little bird
Come hop, hop, hop;
So I cried, "Little bird,
Will you stop, stop, stop?"
And was going to the window
To say, "How do you do?"
But he shook his little tail,
And far away he flew.

One, Two, Buckle My Shoe

One, two,
Buckle my shoe;
Three, four,
Shut the door;
Five, six,
Pick up sticks;
Seven, eight,
Lay them straight;
Nine, ten,
A big fat hen;
Eleven, twelve,
Who will delve?
Thirteen, fourteen,
Maids a-courting;
Fifteen, sixteen,
Maids in the kitchen;
Seventeen, eighteen,
Maids a-waiting;
Nineteen, twenty,
My plate's empty.

Pat-a-Cake

Pat-a-cake, pat-a-cake,
　Baker's man,
Bake me a cake
　As fast as you can;
Prick it and pat it,
　And mark it with T,
And put it in the oven
　For Teddy and me.

Pease-Porridge

Pease-porridge hot,
Pease-porridge cold,
Pease-porridge in the pot,
Nine days old.
Some like it hot,
Some like it cold,
Some like it in the pot,
Nine days old.

Polly, Put the Kettle On

Polly, put the kettle on,
Polly, put the kettle on,
Polly, put the kettle on,
And let's drink tea.

Pussy-Cat

Pussy-cat, pussy-cat, where have you been?
"I've been to London to look at the queen."
Pussy-cat, pussy-cat, what did you there?
"I frightened a little mouse under the chair."

Simple Simon

Simple Simon met a pieman
Going to the fair;
Says Simple Simon to the pieman,
"Let me taste your ware."
Says the pieman to Simple Simon,
"Show me first your penny."
Says Simple Simon to the pieman,
"Indeed, I have not any."
Simple Simon went a-fishing
For to catch a whale;
All the water he had got
Was in his mother's pail!

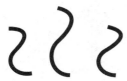
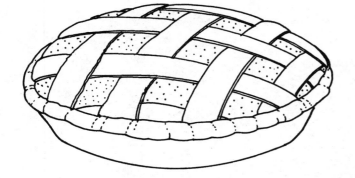

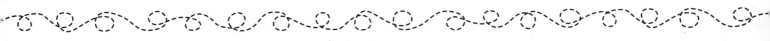

Sing a Song of Sixpence

Sing a song of sixpence,
A pocket full of rye;
Four and twenty blackbirds
Baked in a pie;
When the pie was opened,
The birds began to sing;
Was not that a dainty dish
To set before the king?
The king was in his counting-house
Counting out his money;
The queen was in the parlor
Eating bread and honey;
The maid was in the garden
Hanging out the clothes,
When along came a blackbird
And pecked off her nose.

The Rose

The rose is red,
The violet's blue,
Pinks are sweet,
And so are you!

A Crooked Man

There was a crooked man, and he went a crooked mile,
And found a crooked sixpence upon a crooked stile,
He bought a crooked cat, which caught a crooked mouse,
And they all lived together in a little crooked house.

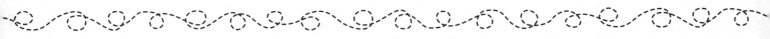

There Was an Old Woman

There was an old woman who lived in a shoe,
She had so many children, she didn't know what to do;
She gave them some broth without any bread,
She whipped them all soundly, and put them to bed.

This Little Pig

This little pig went to market.
This little pig stayed at home.
This little pig had roast beef,
And this little pig had none.
This little pig cried, "Wee, wee, wee!"
All the way home.

Three Blind Mice

Three blind mice! See how they run!
They all ran after the farmer's wife,
Who cut off their tails with the carving knife!
Did you ever see such a thing in your life?
Three blind mice!

To Market

To market, to market, to buy a fat pig,
Home again, home again, jiggety-jig;
To market, to market, to buy a fat hog;
Home again, home again, jiggety-jog;
To market, to market, to buy a plum bun,
Home again, home again, market is done.

Mary's Lamb

Mary had a little lamb,
Its fleece was white as snow,
And everywhere that Mary went
The lamb was sure to go.
He followed her to school one day—
That was against the rule,
It made the children laugh and play,
To see a lamb at school.

A Nonsense Alphabet

A

A was once an apple-pie,
Pidy,
Widy,
Tidy,
Pidy,
Nice insidy,
Apple-pie!

B

B was once a little bear,
Beary,
Wary,
Hairy,
Beary,
Taky cary,
Little Bear!

C

C was once a little cake,
Caky,
Baky,
Maky,
Caky,
Taky caky,
Little Cake!

D

D was once a little doll,
Dolly,
Molly,
Polly,
Nolly,
Nursy Dolly,
Little Doll!

E

E was once a little eel,
Eely,
Weely,
Peely,
Eely,
Twirly, tweely,
Little Eel!

F

F was once a little fish,
Fishy,
Wishy,
Squishy,
Fishy,
In a dishy,
Little Fish!

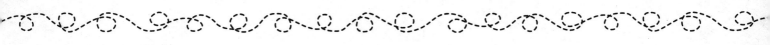

G

G was once a little goose,
Goosy,
Moosy,
Boosy,
Goosy,
Waddly-woosy,
Little Goose!

H

H was once a little hen,
Henny,
Chenny,
Tenny,
Henny,
Eggsy-any,
Little Hen?

I

I was once a bottle of ink,
Inky,
Dinky,
Thinky,
Inky,
Black minky,
Bottle of ink!

J

J was once a jar of jam,
Jammy,
Mammy,
Clammy,
Jammy,
Sweety-swammy,
Jar of jam!

K

K was once a little kite,
Kity,
Whity,
Flighty,
Kity,
Out of sighty,
Little kite!

L

L was once a little lark,
Larky,
Marky,
Harky,
Larky,
In the parky,
Little lark!

M

M was once a little mouse,
Mousy,
Bousey,
Sousy,
Mousy,
In the housy,
Little mouse!

N

N was once a little needle,
Needly,
Tweedly,
Threedly,
Needly,
Wisky, wheedly,
Little needle!

O

O was once a little owl,
Owly,
Prowly,
Howly,
Owly,
Browny fowly,
Little owl!

P

P was once a little pump,
Pumpy,
Slumpy,
Flumpy,
Pumpy,
Dumpy, thumpy
Little pump!

Q

Q was once a little quail,
Quaily,
Faily,
Daily,
Quaily,
Stumpy-taily,
Little quail!

R

R was once a little rose,
Rosy,
Posy,
Nosy,
Rosy,
Blows-y, grows-y,
Little rose!

S

S was once a little shrimp,
Shrimpy,
Nimpy,
Flimpy,
Shrimpy,
Jumpy, jimpy,
Little shrimp!

T

T was once a little thrush,
Thrushy,
Hushy,
Bushy,
Thrushy,
Flitty, flushy,
Little thrush!

U

U was once a little urn,
Urny,
Burny,
Turny,
Urny,
Bubbly, burny
Little urn!

V

V was once a little vine,
Viny,
Winy,
Twiny,
Viny,
Twisty-twiny,
Little vine!

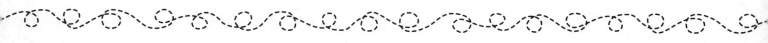

W

W was once a whale,
Whaly,
Scaly,
Shaly,
Whaly,
Tumbly-taily,
Mighty Whale!

X

X was once the great king Xerxes,
Xerxy,
Perxy,
Turxy,
Xerxy,
Linxy, lurxy,
Great King Xerxes!

Y

Y was once a little yew,
Yewdy,
Fewdy,
Crudy,
Yewdy,
Growdy, grewdy,
Little yew!

Z

Z was once a piece of zinc,
Tinky,
Winky,
Blinky,
Tinky,
Tinkly minky,
Piece of zinc!

—Edward Lear

Happy Thought

The world is so full of a number of things,
I'm sure we should all be as happy as kings.

—Robert Louis Stevenson

The Owl and the Pussy-Cat

The Owl and the Pussy-cat went to sea
  In a beautiful pea-green boat.
They took some honey, and plenty of money,
  Wrapped up in a five-pound note.
The Owl looked up to the stars above,
  And sang to a small guitar,
"O lovely Pussy, O Pussy my love,
  What a beautiful Pussy you are,
      You are,
      You are!
  What a beautiful Pussy you are!"

Pussy said to the Owl, "You elegant fowl,
  How charmingly sweet you sing!
Oh! let us be married! Too long we have tarried:
  But what shall we do for a ring?"
They sailed away, for a year and a day,
To the land where the Bong-tree grows.
And there in a wood a Piggy-wig stood,
  With a ring at the end of his nose,
      His nose,
      His nose,
  With a ring at the end of his nose.

"Dear Pig, are you willing to sell for one shilling
  Your ring?" Said the Piggy, "I will."
So they took it away, and were married next day
  By the Turkey who lives on the hill.
They dined on mince and slices of quince,
  Which they ate with a runcible spoon;
And hand in hand, on the edge of the sand,
  They danced by the light of the moon,
      The moon,
      The moon,
  They danced by the light of the moon.

    —Edward Lear

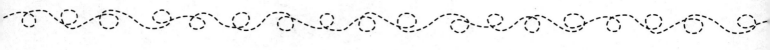

Notes